NEW GROWTH IN GOD'S GARDEN

TRANSFORMING CONGREGATIONS THROUGH MUTUAL MINISTRY

THE REV. MARGARET A. BABCOCK, MDIV, DMIN

**Material in this book is also available
as a downloadable electronic file
with a license to reproduce.**

**For more information
go to www.LeaderResources.org
or call 1-800-941-2218**

ISBN 978-1-59518-060-5

Published and distributed by

LEADERRESOURCES
P.O. Box 302
Leeds, MA 01053
Phone: 800-941-2218
staff@LeaderResources.org
www.LeaderResources.org

DEDICATION

To the people of all the congregations

I have had the privilege to work with,

who have taught me so much

about the power of community and

the presence of the Master Gardener.

-- Margaret A. Babcock

Table of Contents

Section II — The Tool Shed: Resources for Congregational Development in a Mutual Ministry Style

FOREWORD

I come from a long line of gardening enthusiasts. My maternal grandfather planted a garden to provide food for the family table and fresh produce for Clay's Grocery in Shamrock, Texas. My mother nurtured zinnias in the summer, asparagus ferns year round and an ever-changing assortment of annuals and perennials. My own gardening sense came from watching and helping my grandfather and my mother and from my experiments in the Texas microclimates of the Gulf Coast, the Blackland Prairie, and the Edwards Plateau.

When I moved to Michigan in 2001, I inherited extensive perennial gardens with flowers I'd never seen nor heard of and shrubs and trees that were mysteries to me. Slowly, by trial and error and with great patience I've come to an intimate knowledge of my gardens and their contents. I've moved plants around, added further variety, said goodbye to invasive species and incorporated an increasing number of native plants --- all with an eye toward future growth and long-term sustainability.

Margaret Babcock's *New Growth in God's Garden: Transforming Congregations through Mutual Ministry* is an ideal companion for the "congregational gardener" concerned with developing healthy, vibrant and sustainable congregations. Whether a congregational, diocesan (judicatory) or denominational leader, this practical guide will assist you in your ministry. In a time of increased demographic, cultural, and economic challenges for the Church, your spirit will be buoyed by Margaret's clarion call to focus on relationships and unleash a congregation's potential through creative use of community organizing and other techniques.

As a long-time beneficiary of Margaret's deep and profound wisdom, I'm excited to finally have a way to more effectively share her insights throughout my diocese. I heartily commend to you *New Growth in God's Garden: Transforming Congregations through Mutual Ministry* as a tool for your own ministry. May the yield increase in your corner of the Vineyard!

Todd Ousley
Bishop of Eastern Michigan
December 21, 2011
The Feast of St. Thomas the Apostle

CHAPTER 1

WHY MUTUAL MINISTRY?

"…and in the last days it shall be, God declares, that I shall pour out my Spirit on all flesh and your sons and daughters shall prophesy…"   (Acts 2:17)

Imagine with me, if you will, the baptism of a baby. Each one of us has probably been present at many such occasions but, in your mind, pick one baptism which has been special: a son or daughter, grandchild or godchild.

The baptism I am thinking of is that of my first child, Jacob, in St. Alban's Episcopal Church just a few weeks after he was born. We dressed him in the linen gown in which his father had been baptized, but Jake was a big guy and we couldn't quite button it up the back.

The altar guild ladies made him a special little cap and instructed me on the tradition of the baby wearing it on the day of his baptism. They explained how later, I'm supposed to take out some strategically placed threads and pull off the ribbons, so he can carry this cap as a handkerchief on his wedding day. (Jacob's 28 years old now with a steady girlfriend. It occurs to me that I might need to start looking for that little cap!)

And of course, the rector presented us with a candle, lit from the great Paschal candle and preserved by us to light again at Jake's first birthday party. The candle symbolizes this new life given so soon after his birth. I remember all these little details of that baptismal day, as well as the family and friends gathered around us to rejoice.

What I didn't remember so well (and had to go back and look up later), was the description of the relationship with God which gives us new life at baptism. Perhaps, when you think back to your favorite baptism, the Baptismal Covenant is not the thing that pops up first in your memory either. And yet, just as it's important to remember special family moments, it's also important to remember the substance of the sacrament.

What struck me especially, when I went back to read them in *The Book of Common Prayer*, were the promises we all make as baptized people each time we participate in the baptismal service. Just before we let that baby be sprinkled and marked as Christ's own forever, we promise to:

1) continue in the apostle's teaching and fellowship, in the breaking of bread and in the prayers

2) persevere in resisting evil and, whenever we fall into sin, repent and return to the Lord

3) proclaim by word and example the Good News of God in Christ

4) seek and serve Christ in all persons, loving your neighbor as yourself and

5) strive for justice and peace among all people, and respect the dignity of every human being[1]

When I read this list of promises and realize again how this defines the new life to which I committed my baby, I have to laugh at where my attention was focused on my son's baptismal day. What help could an old gown, a handkerchief cap and a quickly burned candle be in the face of such responsibilities? I should have signed my son up then and there with teachers of theology and mentors of mission. I should have enrolled him as an apprentice in service to others.

That, of course, is what is intended, isn't it? As an infant grows up in the shared life of a congregation, the Christian community is there to provide formation, so that he or she will know God's love and will. And the same shared life in community will provide examples of and opportunities for transformation, so that the child will step into the role of serving God, prophesying to God's reign of love with his or her life. Right?

Unfortunately I have to say that, for most of the congregations in which I have lived and worked, this communal support of the formation and transformation of people into God's partners has not been the main focus. While children and adults have been somewhat nurtured in their relationship with God, and while occasional opportunities to explore mission and ministry initiatives are provided, the central concern of most mainline churches remains taking care of themselves by maintaining the institutional life which we have come to think of as "church", i.e. liturgy, pastoral care and administrative tasks.

This is what clergy are trained to do in seminaries. This is what most congregational development programs seek to do more effectively. While the emerging church movement is challenging established denominations with a vision of a more flexible and mission-oriented Christian community, it seems that in traditional denominations we either cannot, or will not, let go of our dependency on institutional stability and the maintenance of what we have been doing for the last 100 or so years.

THE MUTUAL MINISTRY MOVEMENT

Yet we have in our midst a movement which has, since the early 1900s with its initiation by Roland Allen[2], been urging us to think of "Church" in a different way…a way which I have settled on calling "Mutual Ministry" -- although many other titles such as Total Ministry, Circle Ministry, Shared Ministry and Ministry of all the Baptized have been used and other names are being invented, even as I write! While it goes by different labels (maybe because it is still evolving and therefore acknowledging at every milepost a further development of its identity) Mutual Ministry has several benchmarks which form the core of this way of thinking about and being Church.

1ST BENCHMARK: SUSTAINABILITY

The first of these benchmarks is the basic sustainability of the Church. This is often the primary concern of both congregations and their judicatories in times when the expense of maintaining older buildings, the increasing salaries and health insurance for seminary-trained clergy, and the decreasing number of supporting members threaten to close church doors. We need to find a way to survive! But I think it is more than just economic reality which drives the need for local churches to become sustainable. I think it is also a matter of freedom.

The reality is that dependency – having the congregation on life support provided by outsiders – fosters emotional distance and rebellion. In my 10 years of work on diocesan staffs in Idaho and Wyoming, I was distressed by the lack of ownership the majority of members felt towards both their local congregations and the wider Church. It's as if the consumer mentality of our culture has infiltrated our sanctuaries. Christians related to their "institution", especially on the diocesan and wider Church level, as if it were Wal-Mart or the government: expecting instant and cheap services and largely dismissive of those "in charge".

Thinking about this attitude, I realized that this is how my growing children often related to me as their mother! It is a stance of a people without power, of teenagers who have not yet come of age. If the local congregation is dependent on outside gifts for survival, its members will never be empowered to take an equal seat with others at the table. At the same time that they rebel against being told what to do, they will never feel comfortable challenging the status quo. And indeed, in my experience, members of subsidized parishes are never listened to as carefully or seriously as those members whose congregations are independent and add more to the coffers of the institution than they take.

The Church has, for the most part, fostered immaturity and dependency in its lay members since the time of Constantine. At present, the Church's poverty is our greatest gift. As judicatories are no longer able to give congregations what they need to sustain life as they have always lived it, members are being invited to accept more responsibility for the survival of their congregations and, in fact, their denominations.

With responsibility comes independence and choice. We grow up together; to either choose a partnership of equals, or to become extinct as a denomination. Mutual Ministry honors the capacity of every congregation to grow into such maturity and independence. It honors the shared responsibility and freely chosen partnership of a truly democratic relationship between congregations and judicatories. It acknowledges both are needed for the economic sustainability of the Church.

2ND BENCHMARK: EMPOWERMENT

The second benchmark of the Mutual Ministry church is empowerment of all individual members to be mature Christians and therefore full ministers of the congregation, developing the gifts they have been given to serve as partners with God. In the earliest form of the Church, Paul called on all members to recognize that they were indeed endowed with gifts necessary for the health of the whole body of Christ: "There are many different forms of activity, but in everybody it is the same God who is at work in them all. The peculiar manifestation of the Spirit granted to each one is to be used for the general good."(1 Cor. 12:6-7 New Jerusalem Bible)

Many clergy now are necessarily delegating more responsibility to lay members, as churches cannot afford more paid staff. The Mutual Ministry movement, however, does not focus on the perceived gaps of service which need to be filled. Instead, it seeks the skills, talents and even motivation of individuals which may be utilized for God's work. The whole membership is invited into discernment, and then education and training, so that their gifts may be realized and utilized in the community. This formation of all Christians so they can indeed be effective ministers is seen as central to the life of the congregation and an ongoing effort of the whole body.

Early in the history of Mutual Ministry, the belief that every congregation had within its membership the gifts necessary to fulfill God's call came from Roland Allen's missionary work in China. St. Paul's words about financial resources in his second letter to the Corinthians convey this conviction about ministry resources as well: "God is able to provide you with every blessing in abundance, so that you may always have enough of everything and may provide in abundance for every good work." (2 Corinthians 9:6-8) My own experience has convinced me, however, that a congregation may need some outside support and help, especially those churches which have for years been in steep decline, left with only a handful of members. In such cases it is the larger body of Christ which must step in... but not too forcefully. Great care needs to be taken to observe the iron rule of Community Organizing: *"Never do for anyone what they can do for themselves!"*

If the goal is to grow mature and mission-oriented congregations, help must come in the form of teaching, mentoring, and, only in extreme need, providing for particular ministries which are not present. To return to the parenting metaphor again, what is appropriate help to a toddler is not the same support one gives a teen or even a young adult child. Judicatories need to understand and acknowledge that while the era of dependent congregations is over, it is unfair and unhelpful to pull the rug out from underneath parishes which know no other mode of being. Again, partnership in forming Christians into ministers is needed at and among all levels.

3RD BENCHMARK: TRANSFORMATION OF COMMUNITY

The empowerment of all the members of a church leads naturally to our third benchmark: the transformation of the community as a whole. A rigidly hierarchical model of Church cannot sustain a true sharing of ministry. This particular benchmark proves to be a real stumbling block to many who predict that such reorganization will shut out seminary-trained priests and the standards of a professional, paid ministry in the Church.

Personally, I doubt that the transformation of a church into a more democratic model of shared gifts and responsibility will wipe out a professional ministry. I do believe, however, that it will change what congregations are willing to pay for.

At present, in the Episcopal tradition, the largest group of paid ministers is that of "rector" (from the Latin word for "ruler"). In the extreme, these priests are considered by many in the congregation as the professional Christians in the church. This concept, while rarely articulated, allows members of the church to expect a rector to fulfill the responsibilities of the Baptismal Covenant for all of them. It's a "the buck stops here" kind of orientation. If pastoral care is not happening, if the liturgy is uninspiring, if administration does not go smoothly, or if Sunday school is dull and no new people are joining, everyone looks to the rector to fix the problem... or they simply find a new rector.

In a Mutual Ministry parish, all this responsibility cannot fall on one person, paid or otherwise. Instead, the competency this benchmark reaches for is one of teamwork in all areas of congregational life. This is not an ideal that precludes paying for ministry, but it does allow for a variety of choices about whether to pay and what to pay for. Some successful Mutual Ministry churches hire administrators to help in the coordination of church life. Some will pay for theologians to be teachers in their midst, or ministry developers who will help them in their personal and communal development as God's partners. A diocese may choose to fund one or more of these positions for a region or cluster of churches, instead of subsidizing rectors' salaries.

Some congregations will still choose to have paid rectors or pastors but redefine the role to be one of an equal with a team of ministers. In this last case especially, there is benefit for the professional in working with a group of people who care about what gifts this particular minister might have and how to support and empower this person to be the best and most fulfilled minister possible, along with everyone else! (As an aside, it would help greatly to have a larger number of mature and courageous seminary-trained priests and pastors willing to explore the Mutual Ministry life instead of fearing it. This is a group of Christians with great commitment and wonderful gifts who could be an asset to the evolution of the institution, if only their fear of extinction could be neutralized!)

4TH BENCHMARK: MISSION ORIENTATION

Finally, the direction which Mutual Ministry takes the Church as a whole is outward, towards the world, with an acknowledgment that: "The church doesn't have a mission. God's mission has a church".[3] This outward turning begins as members are formed into mature servant ministers and as congregations move beyond lip service to being God's partners in the reconciling and healing work of ongoing Creation. As they actively seek to live out that partnership corporately, then the focus of the Church naturally swings from an inward preoccupation with survival to an energized life of reaching out to others in God's love. This, as Christopher Duraisingh points out, is a profound cultural shift into "a posture of being 'turned inside out'." [4]

Such transformation doesn't happen easily or through the efforts of an isolated or outsider group. It requires a critical mass of members embracing the promises they made to partner with God at their baptism and reprioritizing their communal life to spend resources, energy and leadership on that partnership. This change doesn't leave behind concern for the congregation's own internal life (liturgy, pastoral care and administration)…at least if it wants to be more than a brief flash of ministry in the world's very large pan! Gifts for ministry, empowered by the discernment and education of all the members, deepen the resources and increase the number of ministers available to the congregation in all aspects of its life.

Congregations which are living into Mutual Ministry in the fullest sense of the word, are invariably surprised by the richer meaning of their worship and a wider sense of care for each other. Supporting one another in ministry always seems to release energy for Mission in the entire congregation. (It remains to be seen if Mutual Ministry congregations will have an impact on the evolution of the Church as a whole or even significantly influence the dioceses in which they exist, but there is certainly some evidence to indicate this is happening. See especially the stories of Episcopal congregations and diocese as reported in *Born of Water, Born of Spirit,* by Sheryl Kujawa-Holbrook and Fredrica Harris Thompsett.[5])

The focus of this congregational development book is on helping churches become Mutual Ministry communities, no matter what their size or resources. It seeks a way of church growth which honors local context by moving towards economic sustainability and independence, developing the ministry of every member, building teams to organize and direct the work of the body, and extending the church community into Mission which reflects our covenant with God in Christ. Put more simply, I'd like every congregation to become that holy place which not only provides handkerchief caps for babies being baptized but which also empowers its members, through education, example, and opportunity, to live fully into their baptismal promise to be Christ's presence in the world.

CHAPTER 1 — CONVERSATION STARTERS

Use the following questions to begin a conversation about your congregation's hopes and expectations as you move into a congregational development process.

1) As we begin a congregational development effort, do we have thoughts or feelings about what we want the outcomes to be? Share these with the group.

2) Benchmarks are helpful in providing guidelines for assessing success. Of the four benchmarks mentioned — Sustainability, Empowerment, Transformation of Community, and Mission Orientation — which seem the most important to you? Why?

3) Will any of the four benchmarks present a challenge or even a barrier to the membership of your church? If so, how will you address that challenge?

CHAPTER 2

GROUNDWORK!

> *"Other seed fell into good soil and brought forth grain, growing up and increasing and yielding thirty and sixty and a hundredfold...Let anyone with ears to hear listen."*   (Mark 4:8-9 NRSV)

I'm a lousy gardener. I always thought it was my fault, that I just had a "brown" thumb. But recently, a lesson in a new kind of gardening taught me that perhaps there were ways that even I could succeed in growing flowers and vegetables.

Our diocesan staff had gone up to the Thomas Apostle Center in Cody, Wyoming for a time of bonding, vision casting, and planning. One of our retreat activities was to help the center's directors try out the theory of box gardening that they had just learned from a visiting expert. In Wyoming, the soil is usually acidic and the growing season is very short...so the promise of a truly revolutionary way of growing things was tempting (especially for the cook who wanted fresh produce).

We went to work building wooden frames of about 12 feet square and 2 feet high. Then we put together lattice grids of one foot square which would lie on top of the soil and delineate the planting areas. The theory behind this is to organize the placement of the plants so each has enough room to grow and doesn't infringe on the nutrients needed for others.

And then the revelation: Instead of putting any old soil in those boxes, the gardening guru had left us a recipe for dirt. A recipe! I had never heard of such a thing. In my experience, you just put plants into whatever dirt happened to be lying around. For this garden though, special dirt with ingredients proven to yield results literally laid the groundwork.

Into the long bed of the center's truck went compost, vermiculite, peat moss and who knows what else...until it was almost full. Then two guys with shovels got in and tossed it around until it was all mixed up. This carefully created soil was poured into the boxes we had built, the grids were placed on top and our friends were ready to start planting. That summer, I returned to Thomas Apostle Center to feast on lettuce from a now productive garden. (In the interest of full disclosure, I must say the rabbits benefitted too...but that is another story!)

What I gained most immediately from this gardening experience is a metaphor for talking about congregational development. I used to say that there are six steps which must be taken for a church to be on the path to healthy and sustainable growth (and I mean here not just in terms of the number of people attending but more importantly in spiritual and missional maturity). However, "steps" usually are taken in a sequential and orderly process, and my experience of church work is anything but orderly! I find the organic, rather chaotic image of gardening much more apropos... and here is gardening with a recipe for success, a list of ingredients for us to mix up and lay down as good soil!

The next chapters of this book will be devoted to looking at the ingredients for good soil in a church and how they might be added to the plot in which your congregation is already planted. But in this chapter we will began where I did in my gardening experiment: we'll explore the necessary framework which must be constructed to hold and organize the new Church culture you are creating, and how to assess the context where your congregation is already planted, to determine what proportion of ingredients is right for your congregation.

THE FRAMEWORK

A box frame to hold the new soil is important. It concentrates the new dirt, keeps it together and high enough that the roots of new plants can grow quickly in the looser and more nurturing earth. In the same way, before beginning (and then throughout) a Congregational Development process, it's best to practice some skills which will allow the community to loosen up and nurture the new ideas and experiences which will be introduced. The four communal skills which I find indispensible are:

    1) the ability to converse

    2) the willingness to know and be known by others in the congregation

    3) practicing an intentional connection to God

    4) proactive patience

These four skills are the planks your congregation can use to build the framework needed to contain the new fertile ground you will be laying down.

ABILITY TO CONVERSE

You might be surprised to see "the ability to converse" on this list. After all, almost everyone can speak and, in most congregations, talk abounds. And most of us also listen -- at least to some extent. The problem seems to be not so much the quantity of talk but the quality or, more specifically, that some types of conversing are used more than others. The four types I'd like to consider here are **debate, discussion, conversation** and **dialogue**.

Debate and discussion are styles of conversing which seek to find out what is right. This is very evident in debate, where each person takes the side of an issue and seeks to "prove" that it is correct. In a **debate**, the other side is never convinced. It is only defeated.

Discussion is similar to debate but less intense. As Peter Senge points out in *The Fifth Discipline*, discussion comes from the same root as percussion and concussion. The point of discussion is to hit the issue back and forth until one person's point of view is accepted by everyone else.[6] If you have ever been in a Bible discussion group, you may have experienced this kind of conversing. Usually, the person with the most knowledge (or at least the most reference books) wins.

Win-Lose forms of communication can be entertaining. They certainly help us come to decisions. But they are also, in varying degrees, threatening. In most churches we avoid the tension they bring by accepting what an "expert" (usually the rector or pastor) tells us about our faith. We might also engage in the mild coffee hour chat which skims the surface of our lives, delving briefly into gossip or sympathetic care when circumstances warrant. However, it's only when hot button issues surface (like sexuality, money difficulties, etc.) that we venture to share what we really think and feel. If those values are shared in a culture which knows only how to debate or discuss, there will be winners and losers. The losers will either hesitate to speak again in any meaningful way, or they will simply leave.

In contrast to debate and discussion, **conversation** and dialogue don't produce decisions as to what is right. Instead, they play with ideas and create energy by the sharing of many different viewpoints. As Senge, taking us back to the original meaning of dialogue, points out, "To the Greeks *dia-logos* meant a free-flowing of meaning through a group, allowing the group to discover insights not attainable individually."[7]

Dialogue usually has a focused field or issue, while conversation indicates a more relaxed exchange. Both create a synergy in give and take, birthing new ideas and directions for all involved. This kind of conversing requires vulnerability in participants, a willingness to put out on the table thoughts and feelings and to be influenced by others. In an atmosphere of conversation and dialogue, passionate opinions are shared not to defeat others, but to look at an issue through as many different lenses as possible. In a dialogue or conversation, no one gets to win…but everyone may benefit and grow.

In my experience, mainline congregations use discussion and debate almost exclusively in their communal life, even when they intend to be having conversations and dialogues. Why this lopsided style? Well, for one thing, we live in a culture where winning, even without trophies, is the thing to do. We are surrounded by the competitive norms of our society – just think about the news media and politics. For another thing, it takes much more time in dialogue and conversation to reach group consensus, and our society tends to value quick decision-making and immediate results.

A congregation which decides to engage a more collaborative style of conversing has made a commitment to being very counter-cultural. However, to return to our box garden metaphor, this commitment will be invaluable. It helps us raise our congregational garden above the hard packed soil of judgment and become a looser, more hospitable environment encouraging everyone's participation and growth.

So how do we put this part of the framework in place? Well, in her book on conversation, *Turning to One Another,* Margaret Wheatley spells out some basic principles to meaningful, deep conversations:

- We acknowledge one another as equals
- We try to stay curious about each other
- We recognize that we need each other's help to become better listeners
- We slow down so we have time to think and reflect
- We remember that conversation is the natural way humans think together
- We expect it to be messy at times [8]

These are simple precepts... but very difficult for a congregation to follow unless they intentionally practice them together. In the "Tool Shed" section at the end of this book there are exercises for learning and practicing the discipline of dialogue and conversation. It's worth taking time early in a development effort to

Go to p. 135 for the World Café exercise about structuring conversations and p. 181 for suggestions on how to hold House

explain the differences between styles of conversing, so members can come to agreement about when each style might be appropriately used. However, make sure this is a conversation and not a debate!

THE WILLINGNESS TO KNOW AND BE KNOWN

At least half of my work in the last 30 years has been with very small churches, (sometimes fewer than 20 members). In those little congregations, when I ask members to take time to get to know each other better, their first response is to laugh at me! These are people who have been keeping the church doors open for years together, who often are related and grew up with each other. They may not have seen a new person in church for years and the last thing they think they need to spend time on is getting to know each other better. And yet, as they spend a half hour conversing one on one with each other, delving into stories about struggles and triumphs and revealing the personal "whys" of actions taken in their lives, the result has been wonder at all they did NOT know about each other.

If you are an action-oriented, let's-get-going-on-things kind of person, this "getting to know each other more deeply" stuff may sound a bit mushy and pointless to you. However, reflect on this definition of power which comes out of Community Organizing: *Power is the willingness, capacity and ability to act.*

The willingness portion of this definition is foundational. People must <u>want</u> to do something in order to be most effective. You can guilt people into doing things that need to be done for only so long. (Admittedly, some people so need to be needed that you can guilt them for a very long time... but eventually they die and, believe me, no one else will touch what they were doing with a ten-foot pole!) When members of a community take the time and effort to know each other deeply, they begin to understand what motivates each other. And when people are invited to act out of their motivation, they are affirmed and energized.

One of the risks such curiosity about motivation brings is that the asker must also be willing to be asked. I often find that people resist getting to know others because it means they may have to reciprocate with some transparency of their own. And, of course, once your motivation is uncovered, the connection with a community of people who know you at that deep level and can invite you to act on your values is sometimes scary. A new level of commitment and action to which God is calling you may be revealed. That is a challenge we all have to face.

How does a willingness to know and be known create a plank in the framework of congregational development? Just as the whole point of gardening is to produce healthy, vigorous plants, the reason for a congregation is to produce healthy, vigorous Christians. Encouraging people to act out of their own motivation and energy will not only help us do things more happily; it will empower us become the people we are created to be. For a concrete example, consider the story below.

Mike Mather reports in his book *Vital Ministry in the Small–Membership Church* about how his congregation changed the way they interviewed people in the community who came to them for food. Instead of asking them about what they lacked, church members began asking these petitioners about their gifts and experiences. At the end of these in-depth conversations, which elicited many stories, the church volunteers would ask three questions:

1) "What three things are you good enough at that you could teach someone else how to do it?

2) What three things would you like to learn that you don't already know?

3) Who besides God and me is taking this journey with you? (This question affirms the church's belief that we are never alone, even though people often feel alone.)" [9]

By asking (and keeping track of) what people wanted to teach and learn, this congregation had a wonderful way of tapping into what was really important to these people, i.e. what motivated them. They began to know these visitors in a way that an institution rarely cares about. And, following up on these conversations by inviting everyone to actually use their gifts in the church, they brought new people into their midst and greatly expanded their ministries.

So, how do we learn to relate at this level of curiosity about others without becoming invasive or manipulative? The best exercise I know to move a congregation in this direction is the "relational meeting" of Community Organizing. If you are ready to try out getting to know members of your congregation in a deeper way, bring a group of people together to learn this tool. It is a helpful tool which can be used throughout the development process.

Go to p. 173 for more info on Relational Meetings

PRACTICING A CONNECTION WITH GOD

When I teach deep listening to small groups of church members, we often identify a feeling of energy that results from two people connecting my story to your story. Well, connecting my story to your story and then connecting both to God's story generates even more energy and power! Intentional practice of linking our stories with God's story can provide the momentum to get through difficult patches not only in development work, but in community life as a whole.

Individuals have many different prayer disciplines and various ways of including the church community's ministry and mission in their own daily walk with God. However, the discipline that I am recommending as one of the planks in the raised bed of your congregation is done in and with the whole community. It is a remembering together that you are on a journey with God and checking your values and motivations against God's purpose. One of the simplest techniques for this kind of group prayer is to set all the various meetings of the congregation into a context of conversation about God's story.

Our evangelism group in the Episcopal Diocese of Wyoming encourages people to start each church gathering with one member sharing a story out of his or her life and then asking together:

1) Who is God's family in this story? And then...
2) How are they showing God's presence or activity in this story?[10]

The dialogue which arises out of such simple communal reflection roots the rest of the meeting in an awareness of God's presence.

Another way of connecting the conversation in a meeting to God's story is by using the Gospel-Based Discipleship method of Bible study. The goal of this kind of bible study is not to find the "right" way to read a particular passage. Instead the intent, through noticing our individual reactions to the reading, is to connect our stories with God's. I like to keep the Bible open to the passage that was read, so that the group is reminded to come back and revisit that connection any time during their meeting.

Go to p. 187 for the Gospel-Based Discipleship exercise

The other part of this communal discipline of prayer which is important to observe is inviting the whole congregation, along with God, into the conversation. In congregations with more than twenty members, normally everyone can't be included in the planning group for a development process. It becomes important, therefore, to weave the issues, insights and new ideas which are emerging in the focused group into the full life of the congregation and allow them to percolate with everyone. And usually, the time when the whole congregation comes together is at Sunday morning liturgy.

In the worship service, the sermon is the "teachable moment" for everyone in the congregation. Preachers who are part of the development group discussions may want to include the issues or questions which have

Go to p. 135 for more about the

come up, fitting them into a theological context. However the sermon manages to incorporate the topics, remember that in order to begin a true conversation with the congregation, invitation to response and dialogue has to be built in. This, unfortunately, is not the norm for most preachers. Some preachers are adept at inviting response within the preaching time itself. I like to end sermons with questions which can then be picked up in coffee hour conversations after the services. This may be a good time to introduce the World Café and focus conversation on the question posed in the sermon.

General announcements, whenever your congregation includes them, also work as a time to invite the whole body to reflect with members of focused groups. A quick statement of the issues or questions the group is currently reflecting on and an invitation to think, pray and then talk to those members is often enough to keep the body engaged. Such transparency offers entry points into true dialogue. This is especially helpful if anyone should be upset with the direction a group is taking. It's also delightful when an outsider comes up with an insight which moves the conversation to a new level!

This plank of "practicing our connection with God" then includes working to keep the congregation connected with each other through reflection on an intentional, communal relationship with God. It is a crucial part of inviting the whole membership to be deeply rooted in the One who nurtures us all.

PROACTIVE PATIENCE

The final skill which will complete the raised bed for the containment of new congregational development soil is patience. We live in a society obsessed with getting what we want when we want it. Often this is what congregational development offers – but not THIS congregational development. To develop a congregation in the Mutual Ministry style is to transform a hierarchical culture which has been around for many, many years. Deep systemic change takes time.

How much time? Significantly more than the six-week course that most people are willing to sign up for! It takes at least seven years to effect true cultural change. While this may sound depressing, remember that each of the ingredients you add to your congregational garden will make it stronger and healthier.

The key to patience is to make it proactive. Most of the time, leaders of a congregation live reactively. The furnace blew up? Then get to work raising money to buy a new one. People are no longer coming consistently? Then figure out how to be more attractive to them. This can lead to a frantic pace of simply keeping up with crises.

But when you know you are working toward a long-term goal which will lead to greater health and wholeness, rather than a short-term fix, it makes sense to invest time and energy. Looking towards a future of seven or more years encourages patience with short-term problems. The focus shifts to the evolution of the whole system.

When we are practicing proactive patience, more of our energy will be spent getting out in front of the problems to see how Church is working. Sometimes, what makes the most difference may be a very little change. As Senge says, "Small, well-focused actions can sometimes produce significant, enduring improvements if they're in the right place."[11]

Anxiety, especially about the viability of a congregation, is perhaps the greatest barrier to patience. It may be good to remember here that the gospels contain the story of God's patience with humanity. Fear about the future is not what we are called to, but rather confidence in a future to which God is committed. We may not know the outcome, but we know who is on the journey with us. If we can hang on to this faith, we may find both truth and liberation in this intriguing definition of freedom which Peter Schwartz offers in his book on planning for the long-term future: "...freedom is the ability to act both with confidence and a full knowledge of uncertainty."[12]

One way to foster the patience needed to be proactive and anxiety free is simply to rehearse, at the beginning of every church gathering for work or worship, the fact that you, as a congregation, are committed to that long view of the future. If this feels strange and unwieldy, the AA adage "Fake it 'til you make it" will stand you in good stead.

In the next chapter we will explore getting to the heart of why a congregation may need to change (i.e. seeing the system through the symptoms), but fostering an attitude of proactive patience will go a long way to help a congregation hold onto its commitment to do things differently.

The above "planks" of 1) the ability to converse, 2) the willingness to know and to be known, 3) practicing our connection to God and 4) proactive patience are universals which need to be in place as the congregation makes a commitment to development. Taking time to work on these may be your congregation's first step in the process of transformation. Don't worry, though, if your community is not perfect in these areas. The goal is not perfection but progress. And these four areas will be "in process" for the rest of your congregation's life!

MIXING UP THE SOIL

When the four planks are ready to hold some new soil, then the work begins to mix in the elements which will encourage transformation. Before you begin reading through the next chapters, let me remind you that while I've put these in a sequence which may be helpful (and which I would certainly recommend for a new church start), your congregation may have been in the ground for a while now. The context of your congregation needs to be taken seriously and a plan for development mapped out in consideration of what you have already done and been. All the ingredients should be included eventually, but the amount and sequence for adding them will differ in each setting.

As you move through the chapters, note in the "Conversation Starters" what your congregation has done already in these areas. You may want to revisit and acknowledge work which has already been accomplished or at least started. If you are studying this book in a group, pay attention to where the most energy emerges from your conversations. It's always good to begin where people feel excitement. Think carefully about the personalities and resources in your congregation when deciding which programs to pursue. I'll try to help by describing the pros and cons of different exercises recommended in this book, but remember that there may be other tools you will want to use as well.

Finally, don't be afraid to make mistakes. Fortunately for those of us who work with congregations, development is not an exact science. As in gardening, plants and communities generally want to grow towards health and wholeness. We can make mistakes one year and come back to readjust the mixture the next. The most important thing is to be learning and refining as we go, so that all of our efforts are built on the assessment of what is, or is not, nurturing in our situation and helping us grow into the people God calls us to be.

CHAPTER 2 — CONVERSATION STARTERS

As you and your group work through the following questions, remember that there are no right answers. Conversation is about getting as many different perspectives on the table as possible and seeing what new understanding emerges. You may want each individual to answer the questions silently, mark the scale and then give everyone a turn describing where they see the congregation. (This lets the introverts and less verbal members have a chance to get their thoughts in order and have equal input.) Then open the floor up to more conversation after everyone has had a chance to offer an opinion.

When dialogue seems to be complete, see if you can come to consensus on what actions you might want to try. Remember, there are exercises in the "Tool Shed" section of this book that may also be helpful.

1) In our congregation, how well do we converse for exchange of ideas and the development of new insights (conversation and dialogue) as opposed to pushing for decisions about what is right?

1	2	3	4	5	6	7	8	9	10

Never Happens   **Use conversation as much as debate**   **Got it down!**

How might we deepen the skills of conversation and dialogue in our congregation?

2) Are we aware of our own motivations? How well do we know other people in the congregation and what motivates them?

1	2	3	4	5	6	7	8	9	10

Clueless   **Maybe ½ of us are sharing**   **All motivations are known/shared**

How might we get to know each other at even deeper levels?

3) Are we connecting our conversations about congregational development with God's story? Are we sharing and listening to the wider congregation?

1	2	3	4	5	6	7	8	9	10

Completely isolated   **Some connection**   **Deliberate and disciplined**

What could we do to begin and/or deepen the connections between our congregational development efforts, the wider congregation and God's story?

4) How focused are we on a long term (7+ years) development? How patiently are we pursuing (both thinking about and acting on) a long term vision?

1	2	3	4	5	6	7	8	9	10

Completely Reactive   **Look ahead but don't do a lot**   **Proactive and patiently working**

How can we continue to increase our capacity for patience as we plan and act towards a future guided by God's call?

CHAPTER 3

PLAYING WITH THE NEED TO CHANGE

> *"Then (Jesus)turned to the crowd: "When you see clouds coming from the west, you say 'storm's coming'-and you are right... You know how to tell a change in the weather so don't tell me you can't tell a change in the season, the God-season we're in now."*   *(Luke 12:54-56 The Message)*

When I was a small child and the weather was rainy or cold, my mother would often set up a card table in the middle of the living room and drape a blanket over it. When my siblings and I crawled underneath, we entered into a realm where anything at all was possible. We could have played at any fantasy: monsters from Mars, children lost in the wild, anything at all. What is interesting to me is that we invariably played games in which we pretended to be grown-ups... the very thing that we were slowly, but inevitably, changing into. Whether imitating a mom and dad in a house, Indians in a teepee, or soldiers fighting bad guys from a bunker, we always played the role of adults. In reality we were still children in the house of our parents, but that space under the table helped us imagine what it would be like when we transformed into grownups ourselves. When the game was over and we emerged from under the blanket, I suspect we were a little more mature than when we had begun.

The first ingredient in the new soil we are mixing for a congregation's transformation is "playing with the need to change". For many people (especially, it seems, in churches) change is a dirty word. I've been advised not to talk about "change" but to soften the concept by using words like "grow" or "develop" in order to avoid upset. But the reality of all life is that if a living thing (be it individual or community) is not changing... it dies.

Margaret Wheatley, in her book *Finding Our Way*, makes an interesting point about successful change. She says that while all entities and organizations change, they must choose what will stimulate their change:

"Some part of the system... notices something. It might be in a memo, a chance comment, a news report. It chooses to be disturbed by this. *Chooses* is the important word here. No one ever tells a living system what should disturb it (even though we try all the time)."[13]

Part of "playing with the need to change" is helping congregations see the storm coming and articulate what, to them, is the signal of a need to change. The question is, "What is important enough to the core members of the congregation, that they are willing to go into chaos to address it?"

My experience is that in the face of fear about the future, the communication in a church may be so blocked that messages which are disturbing are not being shared. Basic to this ingredient in the soil of our new garden then, is the ability to converse about difficult, sometimes even painful, realities.

DISTURBING ISSUES

What are some of the storm clouds, the issues or events, which will stimulate a congregation to choose to be disturbed rather than holding on rigidly to unhelpful patterns of communal life? Well, at this moment in our history there are many catalysts alerting members to God's call for the Church to evolve. Most of them are seen, at least initially, as "bad" things which are happening.

Money, or more accurately a lack of money, may be the most widely perceived disturbing force. Especially in many of our smaller congregations, the harsh reality of insufficient funds to hire full-time seminary trained clergy has made people consider ways of being the Church which we never thought possible. Many Mutual Ministry experiments and efforts are a direct result of being pushed out of the comfortable box of a conventional congregation because there is no more money.

Even in wealthier parishes where the position of rector is not threatened, funding for former support roles such as assistant clergy, musicians and secretarial staff may have dried up. In these situations, leaders (ordained and lay, paid and volunteer) find themselves working harder than ever just to maintain a level of church life which is expected by the membership. The demands of regular Sunday services, extra services (such as weddings, funerals, or holidays), and urgent pastoral needs create a tense and internally focused atmosphere. Outreach into the wider community may become secondary or non-existent. Burn-out among those central to the life of the church becomes a prevalent and persistent problem in such situations.

"Rust-out" may be as big a problem as burn-out, in all sizes and types of churches. While burn-out refers to the exhaustion which sets in when too many tasks need to be done by too few people, rust-out speaks to the feeling of futility when work no longer feeds the soul or seems to be serving a purpose.

In many small churches, the ministries performed faithfully by members for years are no longer drawing younger members to replenish the ranks. Feedback and appreciation from the wider community may also be a thing of the past. Altar guilds, acolyte teams, and women's groups often languish. The planning and preparation for beautiful Sunday services no longer guarantees any increase in worshippers and programs may appear to be undermined by events offered in the wider community. Discouragement may become a congregational way of life.

Contributing to money problems, burn-out and rust-out are changes in population which many congregations are experiencing. The preponderance of older people in the pews is noted by many members. I often hear church members lamenting the fact that there are fewer young people attending and even fewer taking leadership roles. Youth programs and even Sunday Schools flounder or are deserted. Even among older folk, the every-Sunday pattern of attendance seems to be dwindling.

Added to population change inside the church is the situation of changing neighborhoods in which many congregations find themselves. Inner city parishes experience an influx of people around them who are of different nationalities and background than the original members. These congregations may at the same time be facing a membership which is moving to the suburbs. In more rural communities, the presenting problem may be that while young people are moving away for education and job opportunities, no one is moving in to take their place. In both situations, the changing neighborhood is a difficult issue to ignore.

All of the above issues can be linked to changes in American culture. This bigger picture may be what the congregation chooses to focus on. It is clear that the norm of weekly attendance at worship and a personal commitment to a formal religion has disappeared in most of our communities. Numerous studies have pointed out the dramatic decrease in commitment to the denominations people have grown up in, and even the number of people who were raised in Church has diminished. So part of the stress within the community may be around the fact that Christianity is not the norm in our society anymore.

While the presenting issues are usually experienced as "bad", there are some catalysts which people will agree are positive. Sometimes a group within a congregation will together feel a nudge from God to take their faith more seriously and they bring that challenge to the wider body. Or maybe a member will respond to a call to a ministry which requires the whole church to look at itself again and reorganize (or at least rethink) who they are called to be together. This often happens when a member feels drawn to ordained ministry but does not, for some reason, want to go the traditional route of leaving his or her home congregation for training or future employment. What will the church do with this "locally" called person? What does it mean to have a deacon or local priest in the midst of a congregation?

Issues which are "positive" usually don't have the power to unite membership as quickly or as thoroughly as threats to the very life of the congregation. However, they should not be ignored as unimportant. Sometimes, the advent of a positive catalyst gives a church the courage to face the negative factors of life which have been ignored for too long!

These issues discussed are just some of the signals that members of the congregation may be noticing which could spring board them into a significant effort of congregational development. Your church may be focused on something as small as a rearrangement of furniture or it may have a diffuse sense of all of these elements. Whatever is disturbing the core members of your congregation, what you do with that issue will make it either a catalyst or just another irritant of communal life. So, the next step is to gather people together to play with the issue!

BEGINNING THE CONVERSATION

Asking you to play with some of the above issues may seem like an invitation to play with a live hand grenade or broken glass! Take heart, though. No one ever dies of just talking about uncomfortable subjects. And that's all this first step is... friends and family members taking time to share their thoughts about difficult issues which they are facing together.

As a leader, your primary job is to cultivate a safe environment to play with these prickly themes. Review the different ways to converse, found in Chapter 2. At this stage, we want to use those forms of communication which encourage sharing thoughts and feelings: conversation and dialogue. It is important that everyone is clear that this is not the time for making any decisions about what to do.

The physical setting is important. Remember that card table covered with a blanket? Something as simple and silly as that can encourage children to let their imaginations go wild. What does it take to help adults step outside their everyday patterns and "churchy" roles? Consider a setting which is more like a party than a meeting.

While I recommend particular events below to begin conversation around difficult issues the church faces, you may have another process which works as well. Consider these benchmarks for an experience which will help your congregation play with the need to change:

1. It should be inclusive as possible. Provide for all age groups, and for all levels of involvement. Don't forget newer members who may have some different perceptions!

2. It must encourage conversation and dialogue as opposed to debate.

3. The goal is to raise awareness and to generate ideas and insights to be shared with the whole group in such a way that these concepts will enter into the culture of the congregation, to be remembered and revisited.

Two exercises I recommend when congregations are trying to add the "playing with change" ingredient to their garden plot are World Café and House Meetings. Both of these exercises limit the number of people talking together at one time, which facilitates conversation. Both can be done in very informal settings and may include food and drink. Having different members host these conversations in their homes carries the bonus of involving more people as leaders and therefore deepening commitment to the process. However, if that doesn't work with your group, don't despair. A little rearranging of the parish hall and/or several Sunday school rooms can also work, with dedicated hosts and hostesses standing by.

Let's take a look at the process, as well as the pros and cons for both of these conversational tools, starting with the World Café.

If you have never been to a World Café event, visualize a large room with as few as three or up to twenty (or

Go to p. 135 for more about the World

more) small tables set up. A deep question is posed and conversations begin taking place in groups of four people seated around the tables which are covered with butcher paper and scattered with bright markers. People are drawing diagrams and pictures or noting important concepts with the markers on the table as they talk. After about 30-45 minutes, the host of the event interrupts the buzz, and asks people to move to a different table.

You will notice that three people from each setting get up and move while the fourth person (the table host) stays and gives the new arrivals a synopsis of what the last group talked about. The same deep question is reiterated and the conversation continues. In another 30 minutes, the host halts the conversation and the mix-up takes place again, conversations going deeper with each round.

At the end of three rounds, everyone directs their attention to the front of the room. Each table host comes forward and synthesizes for the group the important insights and concepts which were shared. These are recorded in some fashion (sometimes in cartoons!) so that the group has documentation of the progress of their collective thinking.

One of the main pros of the World Café style event is that it is so obviously not a business meeting. It's hard to hang on to a habit of debate in such a setting. It feels much more like a card party without the cards! And, if the guests can get the hang of drawing on the table, that also adds to the atmosphere of non-conformity.

The reiteration of the same question, to be discussed three times in a row, invites people to deepen both their thinking and their sharing on subjects. There is sometimes a temptation among those who see themselves as "experts" to simply restate at each table their opinion as the last word on a subject. However, skilled table hosts and good instructions help alleviate this problem.

Another drawback to this style of conversation is that the presenting questions must be very good, i.e. non-leading, yet relevant and deep queries which will illicit real thought from participants. The World Café website has good suggestions for creating such conversation starters. I would also urge the group planning the event to test the question out...maybe on table hosts or members of the planning group. If it doesn't excite conversation in the test group, go back to the drawing board and try again. The question is very important!

The World Café is a brilliant way to try on true conversational skills while exploring issues that can be scary and controversial. It takes a bit of practice before some people are comfortable with the format. A benefit of engaging in this context, though, is that you can use it for many different subjects. (The World Café is a handy tool for mixing in other ingredients of our new soil as well!)

Now let's look at the House Meeting event: As you peek in on a House Meeting which is beginning, you will see six to ten people gathered in a circle settling down

Go to p. 181 for more on House Meetings

to talk. They may have broken out of a larger meeting gathered at the church and be one of several small groups taking place at this time. Or they may be one of many similar meetings which are taking place in different settings and at different times to accommodate the schedules of the church's members.

In the small group, there is a discussion leader who will pose the questions, make sure everyone is invited to talk and generally facilitates the meeting. There is also a note taker, ready with paper and pen, to record insights or ideas. Both facilitator and the note taker will also model conversational skills throughout the meeting, encouraging the group to be good listeners and respectful participants.

Often the facilitator will start by reminding people that this is a session to share thoughts and feelings...not to make decisions or take action. There may be some group norms that are also offered, such as allowing everyone to finish what they are saying before another starts, not criticizing others' ideas, etc.

Conversation begins by asking for personal stories about experiences which relate to the meeting's topic. For example, "Tell us about a time when you felt our congregation's life change" might be the opening gambit. Stories which link the subject to personal experience give insight into each participant's motivation for being part of the conversation. It also anchors the dialogue in the real world rather than ivory tower musings.

After everyone has introduced themselves and shared a personal story, a more general question is posed. In this case a question like, "What catalysts for change do you think our church is facing now and why?" might be used. The conversation now becomes more spontaneous and free flowing, but the facilitator still watches to make sure everyone has a chance to speak.

After about 30 minutes of dialogue around this second question, the session is wrapped up. Reports on the gist of insights and ideas from all the house meetings are either shared with the larger group at this time (if the meetings are happening at the same time and place) or they are gathered by the group leaders and shared in a news article or on a Sunday morning. The important point here is that each participant sees that the ideas they generated are acknowledged and that they are also informed about insights from the other groups.

While the House Meeting format is more formal than the World Café setting, the intentional request for a personal story to begin the conversation helps people think outside of the box. Actually doing the meetings in a member's home, if possible, also reinforces the fact that this is not a business meeting.

House meetings may take less time for the general participant and provide more flexibility for busy parishioners. A house meeting may be done in different settings, at different times, in as little as an hour, while the World Café requires a minimum of two hours with everyone present at once.

The down side is that those involved in House Meetings don't get the variety and depth of interaction with other members which the World Café offers. Depending on the set up, they also may miss an on-site reporting of ideas from all the small group discussions…and therefore the excitement and energy generated by the event.

House Meetings come out of the Community Organizing tradition. If your congregation has been doing Relational Meetings to get to know each other, see the Relational Meetings material on page 180 in the Tool Shed section at the back of this book. House Meetings may be a logical extension of your work.

Both House Meetings and the World Café events require a team of dedicated planners and well-trained facilitators. Recruit your leaders well for these events, plan carefully, and practice the questions you select before launching them. Neither of these events is difficult to do, but both require intention and commitment.

WATCHING FOR WEEDS

Playing with the need to change is a simple, fundamental concept which, if added to the congregation's soil, will stabilize the development process immensely. However there are lurking, even in this most benign of additions to the church's garden plot, the seeds of problems which may threaten the growth and vitality of the whole system.

The barriers to successfully transforming the Church stem mostly from fear. While some would say that this fear is simply resistance to change itself, I have my doubts (as does Margaret Wheatley who says "The old story asserts that resistance to change is a fact of life... But the new story explains resistance not as a fact of life, but evidence of an act *against* life."[14]) The question is: What is making us afraid, and therefore resistant?

I think maybe one thing which scares us about "change" is that somehow this word does not let us ignore the fact that when we grow or develop, something has to be left behind. This didn't seem to bother us as children. We were confident that as we grew into adulthood we wouldn't miss being kids. Our eyes were steadfastly fixed on the change that we, and everyone around us, expected to happen. In our play we practiced (imperfectly and sometimes with mistaken notions of what it means to be adult) the transformation we desired... not looking back to mourn what we were leaving.

Somehow as adults, our orientation to change has shifted and we seem to spend most of our time worrying about what we will lose. Two things seem to contribute to this focus: The first is that we make negative assumptions and take them as literal truth. As Peter Senge points out, "...over time, our personal perceptions can become self-reinforcing and gradually build up mental models, untested assumptions and habitual ways of seeing..."[15] In my experience, congregational life is rife with assumptions we all make about meaning, inclusion, and worthiness. People may be fretting (mostly unconsciously) about losing power and control, becoming marginal members of their faith family. They may be thinking things like: "We just know no one can do a better liturgy than we had twenty years ago. And if changes come, who will be around to baptize my baby or care that I want to be buried to the same hymns I grew up with?" Such background thoughts raise resistance to any change!

To pull up the weeds that assumptions sow means first of all exposing these thoughts as perceptions, not facts. And, the first person's assumptions to test are your own! Developing a habit of exposing your own thought processes in conversations will model a more open way of thinking and sharing. There is a great section in *The Fifth Discipline Fieldbook*[16] which contains suggestions for making our thinking more open and transparent. Prefacing statements with phrases like "Here's what I think and how I got there..." Or asking "Do you see this differently?" can really expose our assumptions and open up dialogue.

The same is true in encouraging other people to be aware of their assumptions. Gently, and with real interest, ask "How did you arrive at that view?" Clarify your own reaction by responding, "When you say such and such, I worry that it means..." While at first these phrases may sound a little mechanical, with practice they become more natural. The benefit of a true give-and-take not shadowed by negative assumptions is worth the attention it takes.

Lack of visualization is another thing which seems to orient adults towards what will be lost rather than what will be gained, in any change process. We can't imagine our congregation looking radically different than our grandparents' church. And because we can't imagine it differently (Remember nature abhors a vacuum!) we focus on our already formed mental models, and dread having them changed.

I don't think people are really so deficient in imagination that they couldn't fantasize a church which is closer to Christ's vision, more filled with the Spirit, and more powerfully and positively influencing the world. I just think we are rarely asked to do this. We make the assumption that someone from outside (who does not know or value us) will impose change on our congregation. And while change is natural and enlivening to all natural systems, no living entity likes to be controlled! As Wheatley says, "All of life reacts to any process that inhibits its freedom to create itself."[17]

The way to deal with lack of visualization and the fear of outside control over change, as with other assumptions, is to acknowledge it and expose it. Even if outside forces cut funding and pressure your church to look at different ways of organizing, you don't have to play the victim. Put on the hero's hat instead and choose to play the game in such a way that everyone is led to greater insight about God's will and love!

Of course, for a group to take control of the game in this way also means group members must commit time and energy to the effort of transformation. And this brings us to another weed to watch out for: the "let's get it over and done with" weed.

Even when members bow to the inevitable, biting the bullet and agreeing to a development process, many people anxiously count the hours until the effort will cease and they can get back to normal. The assumption here is that "normal" is good enough. The expected change in this case is not transformation but a return to the status quo.

One of the reasons that we need to articulate and play with our need to change is so we won't abandon our efforts at the first sign of success. Often, like a patient being treated with antibiotics, we happily quit taking our medicine the minute we begin to feel better. But we ignore the doctor's admonition to keep taking the penicillin to the end of the prescribed course, to our peril. If we give in to the temptation to get back to normal before the meds are finished, whatever has been plaguing us can come back and hit just that much harder in the future. And the medicine will no longer be effective against it.

So too with congregational development: If we work at development just enough so the current members stay comfortable, then we have missed an opportunity for transformation. Somehow we have not truly heard God's call to become more fully God's people. Soon, either the issue which goaded us into the development process will return or another irritant will be with us. If we have not truly grown, we will have no greater coping mechanisms or resources to deal with the issue.

PLAYING AT BEING INHABITANTS OF HEAVEN

In some ways, "playing with the need to change" is the essence of our congregational life. Christ calls us recognize the signs and join him on a journey of death and resurrection, which leads to spiritual development. If we do this well, we grow into the likeness of Christ. We live the life of heaven on earth.

Actually, participating in the worship service always feels a bit like being a kid under the card table in the middle of the living room. In the structures we humans have built under the vault of God's heaven, we play at becoming the people we are created to be, rehearsing our roles as the heirs of God's reign. We visualize the stories of God's relationship with us and go through the patterns of connection and commitment, love and forgiveness. We don't do it perfectly in any denomination, in any particular congregation...but the intent is there. And I am convinced that most of us come out of the church doors on Sunday morning a little more mature as followers of Christ.

In the congregational development garden soil, this ingredient of "playing with the need to change" is just an extension of the game we are invited to play with God every day and in every way. Playing is, after all, the fundamental way we have been created to learn and transform ourselves… to choose who we will be.

CHAPTER 3 — CONVERSATION STARTERS

As you read through the chapters of this book, either by yourself or with a group, consider whether now is the time to add a particular ingredient to your congregation's soil. For "playing with the need to change" the following questions may lead to fruitful dialogue.

1) Have we already shared with each other the issues which disturb us and lead us to consider congregational development? If so, can we articulate what we are choosing to serve as the catalyst for change?

2) If we are at a place to add this ingredient to our new soil, which kind of event or program might be most helpful in our context? Consider how to:
   a. include as many members as possible
   b. encourage conversation rather than debate
   c. generate insights which can be shared and revisited

3) In such an event, who would we invite to be on the planning and leadership team?

4) What "weeds" most threaten our "playing with the need to change"? How can we prevent them or pull them up?

CHAPTER 4

EXPLORING THE CONGREGATION'S PAST AND PRESENT IDENTITY

> *"The way God designed our bodies is a model for understanding our lives together as a church: every part dependent on every other part, the parts we mention and the parts we don't, the parts we see and the parts we don't."*
>
> (1 Corinthians 12:24-26, The Message)[18]

Have you ever been a member of a congregation which changed its location? If so, do you remember how it felt to leave the old space behind and enter the new building? Journeys of this sort can make quite an impression, in both positive and negative ways.

The congregation I grew up in was housed in a traditional brick church with beautiful stained glass windows on the tree-lined main street of our small Midwestern city. My family left the country for two years when I was 11 years old. When we returned, we found the parishioners meeting in the basement of a neighboring church. My congregation had sold its building and was constructing a modern edifice on a larger piece of property near the outskirts of town.

A dear Sunday school teacher had anticipated my return into the midst of our congregation's journey through a wilderness of change. She saved a sun catcher for me: a cross made out of the stained glass windows of our demolished church. When I looked at that sun catcher, I remembered hours on Sunday morning gazing at the pictures and people depicted in those vanished stained glass windows. I remembered how vivid the blues and reds were, even on Christmas Eve when the lights were dim and the candles flickered. Those fragments of glass making up the sun catcher caught and focused my memories of the church of my youth.

A year or so later, when we finally moved into our new church home, there were no stained glass windows. Instead, we had large clear windows letting us gaze out at the beauty of the world and inviting us to connect to the wider community. Our theology was reflected more accurately in this new structure. We all appreciated the greater space and utility of the modern building. But I remain thankful to my teacher who knew that I would want a concrete piece of the old to take with me into the new. She foresaw that I would have difficulty moving into the future if I was disconnected from my past.

Who we are now and who we will become in the future is inevitably linked to who we were before…and this is true for congregations as well as individuals. The component of "exploring the congregation's past and present identity" mixes the personality of the church community into the soil which will nurture future development. Why is this important for us to consider?

AUTOPOIESIS AND CONGREGATIONAL DNA

In the early 1960s, two scientists, Humberto Maturana and Francisco Varela, described a systemic process which they named *"autopoiesis."*[19] This natural law asserts that successful entities continually renew themselves in such a way that their essential integrity remains intact. This happens through self-reference when the need to deal with change is evident:

"In response to environmental disturbances that signal the need for change, the system changes in a way that remains consistent with itself in that environment…focusing its activities on what is required to maintain its own integrity and self-renewal. As it changes, it does so by referring to itself; whatever future form it takes will be consistent with what has gone on before, with the history and identity of the system.[20]

Basically, self-referential growth means that just as kittens can't grow up to be bears and a cherry tree sapling will never become a rose bush, so too parishes must not leave their essential identities behind as they begin to grow. If this concept seems strange in relationship to a church community, we have only to look to St. Paul's great metaphor of the Church as the body of Christ to remind us that congregations are, in fact, living systems. Margaret Wheatley also uses such a concept in her work with the business community, giving out this advice: "A self-organizing system has the freedom to grow and evolve, guided by only one rule: It must remain consistent with itself and its past."[21] (Please note here that "consistent" does not always look like a bigger copy of the original. Butterflies do come from caterpillars and, although the change is amazing, it is consistent because the butterfly was in the caterpillar DNA all the time!)

The challenge to the local church from this perspective is to adequately articulate its essential identity so that any development and growth will be consistent with its nature. But what makes up a congregation's fundamental personality? The short answer is: Patterns of relationships, i.e. the habits, priorities and meanings in your life together.

ARTICULATING THE CONGREGATION'S PERSONALITY

To root a congregational development process in the soil of the church's own DNA requires first and foremost that members embrace the unique and special nature of their community. Just like every individual has strengths and weaknesses, gifts and quirks and personal passions, so each congregation has a distinctive identity. The trick is to get everyone in the community to broaden their view of the church to include the perceptions of others, and then to find a way for the group to articulate this more comprehensive picture.

Here are three basic guidelines to consider as you plan to explore your congregation's past and present identity:

First of all, be as inclusive as possible. I often begin workshops on this topic by saying that the work we will be doing together is like creating a stained glass window. (Yes, this is a recurring metaphor in my life!) Everyone will have a different view of what has happened, as well as how and why an event occurred, in the history of the church. These perceptions are neither all right nor all wrong. Instead, think of these versions of the congregation's story as being separate colors which need to fit together to create the whole picture, as in a brilliantly-colored church window.

The second point can also make use of the stained glass window metaphor. In every church window, while we appreciate the bright and sparkling colors, there would be no real picture without the black lines of lead which hold those glass shards in place. So too, in the history of your church, the tense times of conflict, strife and unhappiness are important to remember.

Noticing the way the community dealt with (and currently handles) the challenges of life is just as important as sharing the fun and joy. In fact, long-buried secrets about incidents which once caused members embarrassment or pain often will surface during workshops where the history of the church is being shared. Sometimes only a few of the older members hold these memories. Other times, many people know bits and pieces of some dark episode but have not talked about the taboo subject openly. In either case, it's important when something which has been hidden emerges, that you name it clearly and allow time to explore and share it fully.

If the experience is very sensitive (for example, sexual misconduct of a former clergy) or of a recent nature, plans for dealing with it after the workshop should be made. And of course, all the members should be informed about what actions will be taken.

The final benchmark of a process which successfully explores the past and present identity of the congregation is looking for the reasons behind traditions, habits and customs. Many times conflicts and even rifts in a congregation occur around decision points which don't seem so earth-shattering to an outsider. When emotions run high and debate replaces all efforts at conversation, you can bet some basic priority or tenet is being threatened.

Take, for example, the issue of whether or not to have stained windows in a new church building: Stained glass windows in the great cathedrals of Europe were beautiful in their own right, but their purpose was to teach an illiterate population the stories of the Christian faith. Their main value to the Church lay not in their attractiveness, but in their ability to convey biblical and historical knowledge to the members.

I wasn't present when the decision was made to use clear windows instead of stained glass in the modern church built in my home town...but I'm sure there was heated discussion about this choice. Even though most churches members are no longer illiterate (and have not been for ages), the tradition of stained glass in church buildings still feels important and "right" to many people today.

Those feelings are important to acknowledge and honor. New ways of thinking also need to be recognized. If a congregation can't together step back and discover the roots of both sides in an argument like this, they risk becoming entrenched in warfare which will split the community. Those roots are sure to be found in the shared identity of the congregation's personality.

To refocus the members on finding the reasons for certain traditions (like having stained glass windows) does not ensure that agreement on a course of action will be reached easily. It does however, encourage deep listening and respect for different points of view. It also encourages the membership to build on what is ultimately important to them in their quest to answer God's call to become God's people. In my childhood church, the importance of the stained glass windows was honored by making sun-catchers which commemorated our history together. Then the membership could move on to live with clear windows.

Possible Processes

Creating church scrapbooks and even designating a congregational historian can help keep a sense of the parish's continuity over time. However, more work usually has to be done to articulate a congregation's personality in a way which will let the communal body grow following its own DNA. This need not be a time-consuming ingredient to add to the developmental soil, however. The knowledge is present in the members. It's just bringing it out and putting it together which is needed.

There are several processes already developed which can help a congregation be inclusive about different views on history, honest about difficult times, and courageous about getting down to the roots of their identity. I'll mention three here, with pros and cons about using them.

SIMPLE TIMELINE

The first and simplest is a timeline as it is used in some Appreciative Inquiry projects. If you are already using an Appreciative Inquiry model, this may fit quite naturally into your process. It consists of calling the congregation together and constructing a timeline: literally a line of paper on the wall with dates and then notes of stories which people will tell about their memories of the congregation. This timeline is then left on display for people to review and add to throughout the Appreciative Inquiry process.

A positive aspect of this time line is the unstructured and informal way it is put together. If you have a congregation resisting one more blasted meeting, it's easy to fit this into a potluck night and make the story telling a fun activity. As leader, you can put key words and phrases on the timeline in appropriate places as members are reminiscing. You may also want to lead into the storytelling with some positive directions like: "Tell us a story about the best things which were happening in this year."

The downside of such informality, though, is that everyone may not be heard. Unless specifically invited, the introverts and shy members may never get a word in edgewise. Also, views that run contrary to a story already presented may not get aired, as there is no specific preparatory work which affirms the value of differing interpretations of history.

Another shortcoming of this process is the lack of any help in interpreting the timeline so a common articulation of the personality of the congregation emerges. You may find that participants spontaneously notice trends or characteristics, such as "We focus most of our mission on children" or "We don't like to ask for money". As leader, you may want to lead the way in expressing such commonalities yourself. Recording these insights allows the members to come back to these insights later when they are seeking to move forward.

Despite these drawbacks, the simple time line approach is helpful if you have a tired and depressed congregation. It also may be a good choice for a second or third round of adding this ingredient to the congregation's soil, when members already have an idea of their joint identity and simply need to remember it and bring newcomers on board. Make it fun and interactive and the experience will energize all involved!

A NIGHT TO REMEMBER

Go to p. 189 for a sample agenda of "A Night to

Another process which I have used frequently comes out of the Alban Institute book, *Discerning Your Congregation's Future.*[22] "A Night to Remember" is a 3-4 hour workshop which guides the congregation in creating a general timeline and then helps distill common threads of the parish's past and present in "meaning statements" which can be used as guides for deciding the future direction of the church.

The timeline in this exercise is again put on the wall of the church, and spans from the time the congregation was born (or at least from the time of the oldest living member) until the present. It is suggested that the events of the world be noted (things like the day WWII ended and the first moon landing). These should be put on the timeline before the workshop begins. Such recording of world history helps people remember church events and also allows for some insight into the relationship between the cultures of church and world.

A notable distinction between this and the former exercise is that after the timeline is constructed and the stories are told, participants here break into small groups to determine "meaning statements". These statements come from common themes they see throughout the history of the church and can be either positive characteristics or negative traits. After the small groups list their "meaning statements", they are shared with all. The whole group is then invited to determine which of these "meaning statements" are most important or illustrative of the church community.

Because the common elements and values of the congregation are formulated and prioritized by the membership, it is much more likely that the congregation will own and use this articulation of who they are as a community. The "meaning statements" are easily shared and can be revisited by the congregation as they plan for development.

This process has the advantage of being fairly short and very inclusive. When I have led it, the participants have had fun and been full of energy. While this workshop still does not encourage differing viewpoints to be expressed during the creation of the timeline, it certainly allows for opinions about the "meaning statements" to be aired, and each member gets equal say in voting for priorities.

THE CONGREGATIONAL IDENTITY WORKSHOP

The final process I have to share with you for discovering the personality of a congregation is a workshop I developed with the goal of creating a map of a communal identity.[23] If you choose this method of determining your DNA, you

Go to p. 193 for an outline of the Congregational Identity

will end up with a visual chart of the congregation. The church's personality is also put into words which will enable you to see it within the context of different types of congregational personalities.

The Congregational Identity Workshop is about twice as long as the other two events mentioned above, so you will need a whole day to complete it. However, it can be broken into two parts done at separate times. My recommendation is that if you choose this two-part option, you schedule them not more than seven days apart. You will also need to make clear that, while all are invited to the first workshop, only those who participate in the first may attend the second. (This is to avoid spending time redoing the results of the first workshop!)

Again, the creation of a timeline is the focus of the first half of this workshop. This time the activity is structured so that everyone is encouraged to share their viewpoints, at any time when they were present in the history of the church.

Eight common questions are asked at ten-year intervals, to encourage stories and remembering which can later be compared throughout the congregation's history. These open-ended inquiries deal with areas of life which Carl Dudley and Sally Johnston (in their book, *Energizing the Congregation*[24]) identified as significant indicators of a church's unique approach to ministry:

1) The context of the church in the wider community
2) What internal ministries were emphasized
3) Partnership in ministry
4) Theology of the ordained leader and the wider congregation
5) Outreach or social ministries
6) Stewardship
7) Evangelism
8) Major weaknesses

As the timeline is constructed, universal themes and ways the church has dealt with these different aspects of its life become evident.

In the second half of the workshop, teaching takes place about the different orientations of churches today, specifically five types which Dudley and Johnson describe: Pillar, Pilgrim, Survivor, Prophet and Servant. Participants are asked to speculate about which of these types their own congregation most closely resembled in their history.

As the present era is approached in this conversation, each participant receives a pie chart on which they can indicate how they see the current personality of their congregation in each of the eight areas. Individually they mark their charts and then share their thoughts with the whole group. No one's opinion is lost, and the dialogue continues as to how the members experience their community.

Finally, the leader of the workshop marks a large pie chart with the tally of the participants' opinions. It's unusual for a congregation to fall into just one "type" of church. Most have a primary and secondary identification. Sometimes a rift is seen between different groups in the congregation which settle into different categories. More often, the whole congregation can see itself in the both the primary and secondary "types" and are comfortable with the complexity of their personality.

An ending conversation, then, revolves around where people can rejoice in the congregation's personality and where they have seen unhealthy patterns which may need to be addressed. Often at this stage, there are some "aha" moments when tension about some issue is clarified by insights gained in the workshop. Confidence in the direction and priorities of development may also surface at this point. Sometimes questions and conflicts will get put on the table which have not been voiced before. As a leader, you will want to note all these reactions. You also should be careful to assure participants that articulating the identity of the congregation is not the end of a process...but just an ingredient in the soil which nourishes the growth of the congregation.

Use the Congregational Identity Workshop when your church has the energy to do some really deep work around their personality. If the investment is not there, go with one of the easier processes and come back around to this one later. The important thing is to regularly look at the church as a living system and make choices around development which are in line with the personality of the community.

TIMING

Just as there is a proper time for everything in the cycle of gardening, it is important to consider when to add each particular ingredient in the cycle of congregational development. On the one hand, the component of "exploring your congregation's past and present identity" is foundational for encouraging healthy growth and response to the need to change. If you are just beginning to consider a focus on congregational development, this element will not only nurture your efforts but also help you decide which processes are most compatible with your communal personality.

On the other hand, there are times when adding this ingredient may be disruptive and confusing. If your church is already in the midst of a redevelopment project this may be the case. Especially if you are targeting a group significantly different than the current members (either younger or of a different culture), to turn attention to introspection may seem pointless and a drain on available energy. If the redevelopment process is going strong and generating new life for the congregation, this would not be the time to separate original members out for an identity workshop.

Even if the development process is concentrating on inviting members who seem to be like the majority of people already in the pews, be sensitive to how the introduction of this element might affect the progress. Often a church will hire a new pastor/rector (or choirmaster or youth leader, etc.), counting on a charismatic presence to attract new people. And often that works for a while. At the height of success, there will be little interest in doing the kind of reflection which this component invites among the whole membership.

In both of the cases above, however, there will come a time to add the ingredient of communal identity exploration. When the excitement of new people in the pews begins to die down and tensions between expectations and priorities begin to surface, you will know the hour has arrived. If this component is not introduced, the congregation is likely to wither once again.

The challenge here is not so much to define the congregation's identity, but to redefine it, now that it has adopted new members. Just as the living system of a family has to adjust when a baby is born or a grandparent moves in, to make room for the unique needs and gifts of the newcomers, so a church must fine-tune its identity to incorporate new circumstances. Engaging in any one of the identity workshops outlined above will help clarify where the congregation is coming from and articulate the challenges ahead. Members, old and new, will define who they are now, together.

Another time to mix in the element of exploring the congregation's identity is when an effort at development has flopped. While going through a discouraging and demoralizing experience, the essence of who you are as community of God and what is of value in that living system needs to be remembered and reaffirmed. At a time of discouragement, this component can inject a positive shot of encouragement to a church's soil.

AND TIME AGAIN

I hope one point that is coming across here is that the addition of this ingredient is not a one-time deal. Just like a single application of fertilizer cannot continue to nourish a garden year after year, so too this component must be added on a regular, preferably annual, basis to be effective. And as the process is done every year, keep two issues in mind.

First of all, check whether the values essential to the congregation are flourishing. More people in the pews may be nice (and help pay the bills) but the true test of congregational development is whether the whole community is evolving in its unique ministry and partnership with God. If a central aspect of the congregation's personality is being ignored (say its focus on children or its creativity in worship), reconsider your strategy.

Secondly, be aware that major system dysfunction will thwart any development process. Sometimes a look at the historical patterns in a church unearths a long existing problem. If there is a serious chronic health issue (such as over dependency on particular leaders or enabling of addictive behavior), take time to grapple with that before committing further to a development process. Every living system has some dysfunctions and if we waited to be perfect…well there would be no reason to develop! However, major disease in a system must be addressed before transformation can occur.

Finally, on a positive note, be aware that this element of articulating the congregation's personality is one of the most potent tools for knitting new members into the fabric of the church. Something special happens when a church family gathers to review who it is and includes its most recently-added participants. The process of sharing what has been pivotal in the history of the community, combined with hearing how the newbies view and value the congregation creates what amounts to an adoption rite. Through this process, new members become rooted in the congregation quickly and securely.

When I rejoined the congregation of my childhood after being gone for two years, I needed help in the transplant process so that I could securely send my roots back down in that community's soil. When new people indicate they want to be part of a church, they need to be grafted into the roots of the family tree. And longtime members of the congregation must somehow tap into and release the latent power that resides in the cells of their communal body, if they are to grow in a healthy manner.

Think of the element of "exploring the congregation's past and present identity" as a kind of root stimulator for your congregation's garden plot. It will help each of the above conditions, energizing and securely grounding the church for healthy development and growth. Used consistently and wisely, it is one of the most important ingredients in our soil for nurturing transformation.

CHAPTER 4 — CONVERSATION STARTERS

As you consider what you have read about "exploring your congregation's past and present identity," use the following questions to help you and your group talk about the timing and strategy of adding this element to our healthy topsoil.

1) Have you had the experience of joining or rejoining a church? If so, what was helpful (or not) to the integration process?

2) Have you ever before considered what our congregation's personality might be? Do you remember workshops which used timelines or have you recently participated in constructing a history of the church which we might look at in light of what we now know?

3) What is the energy level and disposition of your church right now? Will we be engaging in this exploration primarily to boost our liveliness, or do we have the drive to focus on laying the foundation for a development process?

4) After deciding on one of the processes presented in this chapter, or creating another workshop which takes into consideration the standards for a successful exploration (inclusivity, honesty about difficult times and clarity about the reasons behind traditions and priorities), outline the following:

   a. **When?** Set a time and date (even if you have to make it tentative so you can check it against other calendars)

   b. **Next steps?** What needs to be taken care of so the workshop can happen? (check calendar, advertise, practice the leader roles, provide the physical resources like dinner, paper and pens, etc.)

   c. **Who?** Volunteer and/or appoint people to each of the next step responsibilities.

CHAPTER 5

COMMUNAL FORMATION

"A man had a fig tree planted in his vineyard; and he came seeking fruit on it and found none. And he said to the vinedresser, 'Lo these three years I have come seeking fruit upon this fig tree, and I find none. Cut it down; why should it use up the ground?' And he answered him, 'Let it alone, sir, this year also, till I dig about it and put on manure. And if it bears fruit next year, well and good; but if not, you can cut it down.'"

(Luke 13:6-9 RSV)

I was introduced to Mutual Ministry (at the time we were calling it Total Ministry) in the fall of 1985 by Bishop Wes Frensdorff. I remember sitting in a booth at a local restaurant in Williams, Arizona where I had just begun work as the part-time vicar at St. John's. I had a four-month-old babe in arms, and a squirming toddler who was being entertained by his father until the food arrived. Wes had just arrived in Arizona as assistant bishop and was making the rounds, getting to know the personnel and leadership of the small churches which would be his main focus. He began the conversation by complimenting me on my family and asking if I'd like to see pictures of his pride and joy...and then pulled out photos of a bottle of furniture wax and dish soap!

His puns, I later found out, were a notorious part of Wes' repertoire, as was his infectious optimism. But during that first conversation, he also proved to be a major challenge to my way of thinking about the Church and ministry. He called me a "hired gun" and asked what the congregation would do when I left.

I didn't like that label one bit! Here I was, busting a gut trying to be the *wunderkind* of a struggling small church, on track to filling the pews with my brilliant preaching and competently compassionate pastoral care...and this guy had the nerve to question the whole purpose of my ministry. Wasn't I supposed to take care of the church in this little corner of God's kingdom? Who did this new bishop on the block think he was, anyway?

The problem lay not in who Wes thought he was, however. His tag of "hired gun" exposed the root of how I was thinking about my purpose in the role of priest. And after a bit of struggling with it, I decided he was right...I was acting as if I was the only one who could make a difference in the outcome of this church's life.

To be fair, this was the understanding that the people who hired me had conveyed, as well as the bishop and the donor who funded my position. The congregation was dying, so poor that it could not even afford a part-time priest. My job was to turn the situation around, to save them. In the simplest of language: They thought my purpose was to take care of the church and the purpose of the church was to survive.

I found this revelation uninspiring, to say the least. Surely, God was calling us to a more profound meaning and aim than caretaking and preservation. But I was also clear that if the reason for my role amongst them was in question, so was the meaning of the whole church. Thus began a long journey of formation, an effort of digging around our communal roots. We dared to ask the question together: "Who is God calling us to be?"

DEFINING PURPOSE

Donella Meadows, in her book *Thinking in Systems: A Primer* describes the components of any organization as

1) Elements
2) Interconnections
3) A function or purpose [25]

While an intervening action with any one of these components will change the system, the most effective, long term transformations usually come about from addressing the purpose of the whole entity. This is what the parable of the fig tree in the thirteenth chapter of Luke illustrates. The vinedresser wants to get to the root of the problem with the unproductive fig tree, i.e. to revisit and revitalize its purpose.

Take a look at the following picture which is taken from a program called "Rooted in God: Moving from Maintenance to Mission[26] and think with me about how development in congregations is usually approached:

Go to p. 212 for more information about the Rooted in God program

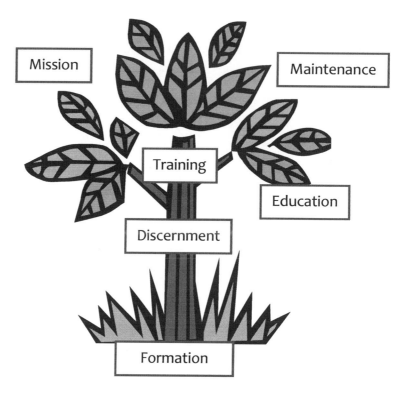

If you are a gardener of my low caliber, the first thing you think of when a tree is looking sickly or is not producing fruit is….water it more! Spray on insecticide! Trim some excess branches! All these are above-ground solutions, reacting to what you see happening above the dirt.

In a similar manner, when we see a congregation languishing, we often try above-ground solutions first. We might try switching out some main elements, like replacing the current rector/pastor with a new one or building a more modern building. Often we will work on interconnections like reorganizing committees and adding exciting new programs, maybe for the Sunday school or the liturgy.

If the church is really stressed and traditional fixes don't seem to getting results or are unavailable, we may try to address elements and interconnections in unconventional ways. This is how Mutual Ministry first dealt with the concern of very poor congregations which needed to learn how to exist without the regular presence of a seminary-trained rector/pastor.

The first efforts in this direction simply sought to supply the missing element. Members were discerned for the role of ordained leader (often in a similar manner to those being sent off to seminary) and then educated and trained close to home. They served without pay, saving the congregation a great expense. The congregations limped on, maintaining their life but not growing in any way. Often the "locally" ordained leaders would burn out, or leave for other reasons, and then the church was right back to where it began.

The next, more successful step was to address the system's interconnections in a more holistic mode. Instead of focusing on one or two members as replacements for an element of the system which was missing, teams of members were discerned, educated and trained together to address ministry in a whole new way. Progress was being made, but it was not a smooth road. Some teams seemed to do better than others.

These teams, as they studied together and then participated in the ongoing life of their congregation in a much deeper, more involved way, often began to see their purpose as Christians in a different way too. When this happened, the congregation's mood and level of vitality increased dramatically. However, when that revelation was not present, burnout and resistance to change continued to be ingrained.

What was happening with the most successful teams was a formation process. As these team participants struggled to reorganize the congregational system, they addressed more than just the separate elements (ministers and ministries) which were needed. They went further than simply exploring and reorganizing their interconnection and relationships with each other. Instead, these groups got down to the very roots of why they were sticking together as Church, i.e. their communal relationship with God. As they met together on a regular basis for prayer and study, they found the room they needed to discover the common and fundamental purpose to which they were being called.

You may wonder about the importance of purpose. You may think that, of course, everyone is on board with why they are a church. But if you did a survey right now in your congregation, you might be surprised at the different answers given when asked about the function of church. (The answers I receive when asking that question often indicate a pursuit of institutional stability, having very little to do with the Kingdom of God and our part in God's plan for creation.)

How can we get down to the level of roots in our congregations? How can we learn together to hear, articulate and follow the purpose to which God has called the Church? How do we even create a safe space in which these kinds of deep questions can be asked? That is the goal of communal formation. Communal formation is a primary ingredient for the development of a congregation and will affect the whole church system in the most direct way.

BENCHMARKS OF FORMATION

I look for four qualities in any formation program to judge whether it will be helpful in articulating or revitalizing a congregation's purpose. I want to know if it is 1) communal, 2) asking "Who is God calling us to be?", 3) taking time, and 4) keeping connected to the whole.

COMMUNAL

It is worth saying again that the formation which we are talking about in this chapter is the formation of the community, not just individuals. While members of the congregation may have had an experience of intense spiritual direction which helped in their own development as Christians, very few of us in the church have engaged as a group in this exercise. And frankly, it's much harder to commit to listening together for a purpose which fits everyone's needs and gifts, and our common relationship with God.

As difficult as it is however, I believe the formation of a congregation is possible. I have faith that members (not just pastors/rectors) are called to belong to particular communities. Our true natures, gifts, and individual relationships with God blossom in such settings. Experience has shown me that individuals develop as the congregation develops. In formation processes, participants often grow in confidence and conviction, becoming stronger followers of Christ and leaders in ministry... frequently in areas in which they had no idea they were gifted!

But it can be an intense process, and not all of the members (even in very small churches) may be able to commit to it. My rule of thumb is that for a formation process to be truly communal there must be a critical mass of church members attending. This means that there must be enough participation to affect the way that the whole system thinks and feels about its purpose.

I used to give ten percent of the average Sunday attendance as the formula for achieving such critical mass in a formation process. While this is a good approximation, attention also needs to be paid to the place of the participants in the overall system of the congregation. If you have twenty percent of the members involved, but no elected leaders or main contributors, it will be much harder to influence the function of the whole. So, as you begin a formation process, invite everyone, but be sure to target with a personal appeal those you know are the formal and informal movers and shakers.

ASKING "WHO IS GOD CALLING US TO BE?

Formation is often confused with Christian education and, if marketed as such, will inevitably be disappointing. Most adults in American culture equate education with learning facts. While new material is often part of formation programs and can be quite exciting and revelatory to participants, the focus of formation is not on gaining knowledge. Instead, the point of formation is to ask "Who is God calling us to be?" and to find the answer within the community.

Because of this orientation, a good formation program spends a lot of time processing information in the group. What individuals think about, what they care about, and how they fit the facts about church history, theology and spirituality into their lives is more important than the information itself. A lot of conversation and dialogue takes place, but there is no room for debate. Obviously, people need to be told this up front.

Most formation groups must be guided in the practice of sharing non-judgmentally as well. If you have already introduced techniques for conversing in your congregation, you will be well ahead of the game here! If not, then leaders will have to work harder at helping participants fine-tune their dialogue skills.

Reminding folks of the function of formation may also need to occur from time to time. This will be especially important if members of the group grow impatient with the lack of didactic teaching (as in, "Just tell us what the right answer is!"). If you have a group which is depressed and unsure of itself, there will be a temptation for the leader to cave in and tell them what he or she thinks, before the group has a chance to find or form their own opinions. Patience, that great but undervalued virtue, is needed to allow the formation process to evolve.

TAKING TIME

This brings us to the issue of "time". One of the indicators of a good formation program is that it does not rush towards resolution. A good deal of anxiety about the process can be alleviated with a time line which encourages participants to settle in, get comfortable with the group, and take the time needed for thoughtful responses.

I have found that 6-12 months are optimum for the best formation programs. Those that go on for years are even better. (Remember the story in Luke: The vinedresser wanted at least a year too!)

This ideal of a long-term commitment is contrary to the best current advice we are given about programming in the church. Six weeks, it is said, is the absolute longest volunteer commitment which people can make in our hectic world. However, congregational development which will result in truly transformational change is not a quick fix. Like a "couch potato" trying to get fit, only long-term commitment to diet and exercise will change body mass and composition. There are no magic pills, even for the church body. In my experience, all Christians (lay and ordained) have the capacity to do this work, once they understand no one else can do it for them.

There are ways to approach the time commitment, however, which help people embrace it. As mentioned before, energy is often generated in the workshops dealing with congregational identity (see Chapter 4). You may be able to channel that burst of vigor into a formation program if it follows on the heels of the workshop. The prospect of spending half a year with the same group will not look so daunting, if people are feeling connected through a previous positive experience.

You also may want to gently ramp up to the formation program by some real education on how the system of the church is currently working. One of the best six-week programs for this is the Episcopal Divinity School's course "Wade in The Water" by Dr. Fredrica Harris Thompsett[27]. This video series invites conversation about the historical and present state of the church. It makes a good precursor to a more in-depth formation process.

KEEPING CONNECTED TO THE WHOLE

Whatever formation program you choose, be aware that how you dig around the roots is just as important as any outcome. It's important to be transparent about what the formation group is doing. It helps to be connected enough to the whole community so that they feel a part of, and therefore supportive of, this work.

Staying connected is not as difficult as it may seem. All it takes is extending the conversations of the formation group into the wider congregation. One group did this by reporting during the announcements, at every Sunday service, about what subjects and themes they had been discussing in the formation program that week. This gave everyone permission to carry on the conversation during coffee hour.

Other groups have set up short Sunday world café conversations which use the same questions the formation group has encountered during the week.

Go to p. 135 for more about the World

Especially if formation group members take the role of table hosts, this encourages the participation and inclusion of the wider group. One church which used this World Café method found that it also helped increase the competence of the whole congregation in having conversations instead of debates... and that in turn facilitated the work of the whole congregational development effort. They kept up the Sunday cafés long after the formation program was completed.

Newsletters and bulletins may also be used to connect the work of the formation group to the greater congregation. Their limitations, however, are severe. With such vehicles, there is no general forum for feedback or differing opinions to influence the smaller group. Therefore articles may either be ignored or worse, create the impression of an elite group deciding the direction the whole church will go... the exact opposite of what communal formation intends.

COMMUNAL FORMATION PROGRAMS

Below are four examples of programs which fit the criteria for communal formation.

ROOTED IN GOD: MOVING FROM MAINTENANCE TO MISSION

Most programs which bill themselves as church development have some components of formation in them. My observation is that many fall short by not digging deeply enough around the roots, i.e. not being clear and aggressive about the formation component. I dealt with this in my work with the Episcopal Church in Idaho (many years after the story I told about Arizona!) by creating a formation program, specifically with very small churches in mind. Indeed, the congregations I was working with helped create "Rooted in God: Moving from Maintenance to Mission"[28]. Later it was used to good effect in pastoral sized churches (50-200) as well.

Go to p. 212 for more information about the Rooted in God

Because this program was developed with communal formation as its goal, it intentionally helps participants ask the questions, "Why are we together?" and "Who is God calling us to be?" It links those present-day inquiries back to the history of the Church and how people in different times have answered them. Of course, conversation about how history illuminates and affects the present-day situation of the congregation becomes the creative edge to these sessions.

Participants also explore the central concepts of Benedictine community: obedience, stability and transformation. Structured exercises provide practice in applying these ancient ideas in the modern congregational setting. As dialogue takes place around the experience, as well as around the ideals, participants begin to see unfolding possibilities.

Rooted in God: Moving from Maintenance to Mission is a downloadable resource published by LeaderResources.[29] One of its advantages is that it is very affordable. The course itself can be purchased online and then as many copies run off as necessary. There are three recommended books (all in paperback) which also need to be acquired for each participant. Any number of people can participate.

This is a program which assumes that formation takes time to integrate into life. It recommends doing its two hour sessions every two weeks. The whole program takes about six months to complete. (It includes a "Rule of Life" workshop which addresses another ingredient in our garden plot, which you will read about in the next chapter.)

Go to p. 218 for more info about Rule of Life

The major drawback to *Rooted in God* is that some people find the non-directive style unsettling. This may be a problem best addressed through clearer explanation of the differences between an education program and formation program. However, there are people who have a great deal of difficulty with the lack of didactic teaching. If such members are in the majority, the open-ended nature of *Rooted in God* may prove too challenging.

LifeCycles

LifeCycles is the quintessential communal formation program, and probably should be called a "process" rather than a program.[30] The theory behind the LifeCycles structure is that participants will encounter the biblical, historical and spiritual life of the Christian community in a regular rhythm of gathering and studying together. Out of that experience they will begin to articulate their own sense of partnership with God.

While *LifeCycles* is even less directive than *Rooted in God*, it does have a well-defined overall structure. The suggested biblical readings take participants pretty much through the Bible, and also include some unorthodox Christian writings such as the Gospel of Thomas. Each session consists of a ritualized opening, readings of Church history and the Bible and then exercises and conversation. It is suggested that different prayer experiences be part of each gathering, as well as sharing a meal or snack.

When asked how long a commitment the *LifeCycles* program requires, there are two answers. The first is six weeks, which is the length of each unit. This is quite comforting to those with hectic schedules who feel that they can't commit to more than six weeks at a time. However, it would be a misleading to congregants to let them think that six weeks is the extent of the commitment.

Go to p. 217 to see an overview chart of topics in LifeCycles

Each unit is part of a cycle of six units. Each cycle then, if the sessions were done consecutively, would take 36 weeks. And there are to date, three cycles completed with one or two more in production. Even if the group were to commit to finishing one cycle a year, they would be involved in *LifeCycles* for longer than any of the other formation programs offered here. (And then a group can go back and do the same cycle over again, gaining deeper understanding and wisdom.)

To commit to *LifeCycles* is to commit to ongoing communal formation. The smaller units make it convenient to break the process up into manageable bites...many groups break at holidays and in the summer. The intent, though, is to form groups which will live into the community life of the program for many years to come. This is one of the greatest strengths of the *LifeCycles* process.

The Episcopal Diocese of Northern Michigan has utilized LifeCycles as the backbone of their formation program. Through it, they have called together and educated teams for ministry which have been very successful and vital. You may want to read more about their story in Kevin Thew Forrester's book *I Have Called You Friends*[31].

Most mainline, traditional congregations can't jump right into *LifeCycles* without some preparatory work. Sometimes the previously-mentioned video program "Wade in the Water" from Episcopal Divinity School is enough to get people off and going. Sometimes *Rooted in God* gives enough of the formation experience in a little more focused and directed way to get a group started. (And because of this, *Rooted in God* is included as a free supplement to the *LifeCycles* program.)

It is my opinion though, that if the congregation gets excited about *LifeCycles*, communal formation will take priority as the main tap root for the life of the church , providing healthy input into the system for years to come.

APPRECIATIVE INQUIRY

A development program which has attracted much attention in recent years is Appreciative Inquiry (AI). While not initially created to be used in congregations, there are variations now being offered exclusively to leaders in the Church. If you have not worked with AI before, the flow chart and description in the resource chapter will give you a general idea of the process. Let me list here some pros and cons of AI as a formation program.

Go to p. 214 for more information about AI – Appreciative

Appreciative Inquiry's main goal is to articulate the greatest strengths of an organization and then invite people to plan their future around those positive attributes by creating "provocative propositions". (These "provocative propositions" then drive the development of the institution, and we will explore them more in the next chapter). AI achieves the benchmark of being a "communal" process by going to the people involved (the stakeholders) and asking them to tell stories which ferret out these assets.

Because of this focus on the positive aspects of a congregation, and the firm avoidance of negative issues, AI is especially appropriate for depressed and tired congregations. When church communities have forgotten the joy of living together, discouraged about their size or daunted by issues of survival, it may seem impossible to generate energy for formation. A team of people gathering stories about the best experiences of individual members reminds everyone that there are indeed solid reasons for hanging together. Calling the group to form a vision of the future grounded on meaningful and happy capabilities unleashes a vigor that potentially drives the development process.

The communal formation benchmark of "keeping connected to the whole" is accomplished by AI in the inclusiveness of its story gathering. All the stakeholders, even the newest or most outlying members, are invited to contribute. Indeed, in the best AI efforts, even community members outside the church are interviewed to determine how the congregation's strengths are perceived by those around it.

Taking a lot of time to process the information gathered is not a strong point of AI, but in general the agenda proceeds at a pace which makes conversation rich and productive. While some methods include workshops which shorten the time requirements, the style which uses individual interviews is best for a formation process because it honors the "take time" benchmark.

The biggest drawback to AI as a formation program has to do with neglect of the church as a system. While the creation of a team of leaders who can work together creatively and productively is assumed by this method, there is no direction as to how this might be done. And because the AI process itself is so positive, any negatives in the current organization of the church are not addressed.

If the congregation's system is flawed, the positive attributes which are foundational may still have difficulty flourishing. To address this weakness, supplemental learning done around how to converse instead of debate will lay a solid foundation for team work. The leaders of an AI program may also want to include some direction on redefining power and leadership, before progressing to the end product of "provocative propositions". Without such preparations, work on those propositions may never go forward. (This subject matter might be borrowed from the next process considered: Community Organizing.)

Overall though, Appreciative Inquiry is a process which, by taking seriously the best stories the congregation has to offer, reminds the church that it is blessed and called to be God's family. While the energy generated by the conscious connection with its best self needs to be directed and focused, many congregations will find this the most helpful choice for their formation.

COMMUNITY ORGANIZING

Like Appreciative Inquiry, Community Organizing (CO) was not initially developed as a congregational formation program. Indeed, its greatest strength lies in building up new communities or helping a group reorganize to use the gifts and talents of all its members. (We'll look at this aspect of CO in the chapter which explores Systemic Reorganization.)

However, as in all living systems, the relationship between purpose and the connections among the elements of the whole is close and vital. It is possible to use the fundamental tools of CO to get at the congregation's wisdom about who God is calling them to be, and empower them to move in that direction. The skills which CO teaches a group about how to talk with each other, how to vision together, and how to include all in a partnership focused on common goals, unleash a great energy for progress.

If we consider the benchmarks of a good formation program, Community Organizing meets most of the criteria. The foundation of CO is the redefinition of power and leadership in a more democratic and egalitarian understanding than most of us employ. Therefore, all of the tools which are used (relational meetings, house meetings, research actions and general assemblies) aim toward transparency as well as involvement of all the members in the work that is being done. It is indeed a conscientiously communal effort, connecting and grounding its work in the whole community. CO teaches how to vision and work as a team.

A section about Community Organizing begins on

It also honors the ideal of taking time. The primary tool of CO, relational meetings, is similar to the Appreciative Inquiry interviews in that they generate meaningful stories in a non-threatening, one on one meeting. Instead of limiting these stories to the best experiences of a person, relational meetings seek to plumb the depths of motivation and leadership capabilities in an individual. A team of parishioners trained in relational meetings can, over a period of several months, connect with the majority of the congregation and begin to appreciate the depth of resources and the direction of call which exists in the community.

And then the real work begins: Knitting together individuals' motivations into goals which point to a vision, and inviting everyone to connect at their own level of interest and leadership. Such work takes time and perseverance. This commitment to connecting with the whole community, however, is another benchmark in a good formation program. CO not only allows for it. CO insists on it.

The hardest benchmark for CO to claim is that of "asking what God is calling us to be". An orientation of listening to God is not necessarily what community organizers emphasize in their training or in their work. However, the long tradition of religious organizations involved in CO, as well as the number of faith-oriented people in the leadership of these groups, has given CO a solid theological foundation. When using CO in a congregation, it is not hard to find resources which help with tying this process to the value structure of a church. One of the best books to consult is Robert Linthicum's *Transforming Power: Biblical Strategies for Making a Difference in Your Community*.[32] A book study before or during a CO process, as well as sermons which connect our stories with God's story will ground a COformation program in God's calling.

Congregations may want to use CO as their formation program especially if they are larger and need to include many people at different levels of involvement. In traditional congregations, though, the biggest barrier to this kind of formation will be the current powers in place. Make sure the rector/pastor and other current leaders are part of the initial planning team and are in tune with the fundamental redefinitions of power and leadership on which CO is based.

UNBINDING THE ROOTS

I have offered a metaphor of congregational development as building a box garden and filling it with new soil to nourish the Church. However, the component of "communal formation" which is essential to this process may need to be described in more vivid and violent terms for most of us in mainline churches. Think of it this way:

If you are starting a new church from scratch, you are planting a seed in your new garden plot which will be able to absorb all the wonderful nutrients that you have carefully folded into the dirt, including "communal formation", with no problem. But those of us in already established churches, with long histories of habits and policies and assumptions, are more like greenhouse trees which have been raised in tubs.

My husband and I planted eleven trees in our yard last summer and three lavender bushes. The nursery owner told us that when we took the trees out of their tubs, we would have to check to see if they were root-bound, i.e. had roots tangled together and ingrown, conforming to the shape of the pot. If so, she advised us to not only pull the roots apart, but to slash the tangle with a razor edge to make sure they would spread out into their new and limitless ground.

We carefully followed her directions, with some trepidation, on the eleven trees. Sure enough they all prospered, showing new growth before the snow began to fly. We did not, however, think to pull apart the lavender bushes' roots. Those three bushes perfectly maintained their shape and color… and grew not one little bit. No amount of fertilizer or water or talking to helped at all. Today, they look exactly like they did when we put them in the ground seven months ago.

Next summer, we will dig up the lavender bushes, pulling and cutting at their roots, before replanting them. In established churches, a similar process must occur. The fundamental purpose of the church must be exposed and pulled apart so people can own it and embrace their part in the congregation's calling. Only then will healthy nutrients, the elements and interconnections of the system, be able to affect the whole life of the church… and only then will growth take place.

If you notice unusual resistance to "communal formation" in your congregation, consider how root-bound the church may be and how strong an aversion any system has to such disruption. It may be a good idea to add both the elements of "playing with the need to change" and "exploring the congregation's past and present identity" before attempting this one. Reminding people of why it will be good to get out of their tub, as well as reassuring them that the essential nature of who they are will not be destroyed, allows for this ingredient to be embraced more enthusiastically.

CHAPTER 5 — CONVERSATION STARTERS

At this point in the book, you are beginning to realize that congregational development is not just one program or even a couple of different programs that you use to "make" the Church grow. To commit to congregational development is to begin the creation of an environment which is conducive to the transformation of the community. This can be an exciting revelation to some and a perceived threat to others. Check in with members BEFORE you begin to promote communal formation, the most in-depth and potentially agitating ingredient of congregational development, to gauge their level of receptivity. Communal formation is the one addition to the garden which needs the most explanation and preparation, if it is to impact the system.

1) Are we ready for communal formation?

| 1 | 2 | 3 | 4 | 5 | 6 | 7 | 8 | 9 | 10 |

1—I hate the idea of changing anything around here.

5—I know we need to dig deep, but hope not to be disturbed.

10—Bring it on! God has something great in mind for us!

Where are most of the members of the congregation on this scale? Where are you? What dynamics do you expect to emerge if you go forward with communal formation?

2) If the majority of the members are at 5 or below on the above scale, how might you encourage a more positive attitude towards a communal formation process?

3) Looking at the benchmarks for a communal formation program, do you know of other programs that might fit the bill? Talk about the pros and cons of the reviewed programs and any others which meet the criteria. Which is the best fit for your congregation?

4) Who will be in the core group which will make a communal formation program work? Could you or members of your study group meet with these people and see how receptive they are at this time? After you meet with them, discuss concerns or questions which arose and decide together how you will address these.

5) Lay out a timeline for the communal formation programs to share with everyone, but only after deciding if this is the time, what program you will do, and who will most likely be in the core group. Receive feedback and tweak as necessary and possible.

CHAPTER 6

A PLAN TO LEARN

"(Jesus) began to speak, and taught them, saying:

Blessed are the poor in spirit, for theirs is the kingdom of heaven.

Blessed are those who mourn, for they will be comforted.

Blessed are the meek, for they will inherit the earth.

Blessed are those who hunger and thirst for righteousness, for they will be filled.

Blessed are the merciful, for they will receive mercy.

Blessed are the pure in heart, for they will see God.

Blessed are the peacemakers, for they will be called the children of God.

Blessed are those who are persecuted for righteousness' sake, for theirs is the kingdom of heaven.

Blessed are you when people revile you and persecute you and utter all kinds of evil against you falsely on my account. Rejoice and be glad, for your reward is great in heaven, for in the same way they persecuted the prophets who were before you."

(Matt. 5:2-11, NRSV)

When I planted my first real garden, I thought it would be rather like building a little model city out of Legos. I planned it out when the winter chill was still in the air. I laid out the various beds in my mind and saw them complete as in the pictures of the plants on seed packets or the memories of my mother's fantastic garden in the fertile soil of Iowa. Then, as the weather warmed, I gave myself a head start by buying small plants already started in the greenhouse. I put on the compost, set out my miniature flowers, herbs and vegetables, and waited for my winter dream to produce itself. Ha!

In reality, the experience of planting and tending a garden is much more like engaging in a long-term relationship than doing construction on a carefully-controlled building site. All the planning you do can be (and usually is) undone by events and circumstances outside your control. You have to stay in touch, not just doing maintenance but actively watching, intervening and sometimes just letting developments take place, if the relationship is going to flourish.

Take, for instance, rabbits. When I planted my garden, I carefully put in marigolds because I had read that these flowers discourage pests. I was thinking of the insect variety when I made my plans. Because this particular garden plot is right up against the front door of my house, I wasn't worried about four-legged critters. I figured they would be frightened away by the daily comings and goings of people.

A very bold mother rabbit, however, discovered that we were not carefully watching the juniper bushes which frame the garden. She made a burrow and four baby bunnies became new inhabitants of our space. My husband discovered the little family and spent some time tramping around the bushes to see if any permanent damage was being done. This activity was evidently enough to make the mother rabbit anxious and, to our relief, the bunny family disappeared.

Our relief was short-lived. We discovered four tiny fluff balls of rabbit under the hose holder, right up against the house. Now we had a real dilemma. If we moved the hose at all, those darling little bunnies would be crushed. We watered by hand for a week until once again the fur balls disappeared. Whew!

But then we realized the whole rabbit family had turned up even closer to the front door in a series of cement blocks which formed a little wall. (Mama Rabbit evidently thought it looked like a bunny condo!) And now those kiddos were old enough to eat things…like my basil and tomatoes. What to do? My values were in conflict: fresh food or wild animals? Fruit of my labor or delight of my eyes? I gave in and decided to spend the summer watching the rabbits grow up.

My cats and I had a ball peering out the front windows, watching those bunnies play. And I found that, much to my relief, the only thing they wanted to eat were the marigolds. They demolished those flowers, ate every last bloom. But by the time they had finished stripping the blossoms, all four babies had grown big enough to move out on their own. The whole family relocated themselves to the back yard wilderness area.

In a month, my marigolds came back more beautiful than anything else in my garden. I have never seen such hardy blooms, such vibrant color. The rabbits left me an autumn gift which, along with the delightful hours of watching them play and grow, more than made up for their summer residence.

Now all garden disturbances don't have such a happy ending. (I'm not sharing here about the mold on the tomatoes or the mint that threatened to escape all containment barriers.) The point is that I was not in control. Planning only took me so far and then I had to learn to interact with what nature was introducing. Sometimes the relationship was much more fun than anything I had planned. Sometimes it was just a pain to live with. When I was patient and reflective enough to pay attention, however, it always taught me something.

PLANNING AS LEARNING

I was taught to think of planning in the church as an exercise in controlling the future. In my experience, strategy groups came together to assess resources and the strengths and weaknesses of their congregations. They would then logically lay out a blueprint for the next 5 years. None of these plans were bad or completely useless, but for the most part the design got scrapped before the first 6 months were up. Life just happened. Key people left. New members brought gifts that hadn't been expected. Cultural shifts interfered.

The planning was not wrong or flawed. Our perspective about planning, our attitude of control, is what did us in. The reality of the future is that it cannot be dictated. As the rate of change increases with developments in technology, communication, and a changing society, our lack of control becomes more and more evident. And therefore, the goal of planning needs to shift from control and manipulation to relationship and learning.

Gerald Harris, author of *The Art of Quantum Planning* says, "The reason to plan… is to create an interactive and continuous learning process that will strengthen the adaptability of the organization to a changing environment."[33] In other words, planning for congregational development is a lot like my garden relationship. Insisting on a strategy which is too rigid and detailed may be more than merely frustrating. Such dependence may lead us to miss the gifts of the unexpected.

So how can we tweak our planning processes to not only cope with the unknown, but to actively seek out unexplored regions as fertile fields of potential vitality? What gardening skills are necessary in the new land of the future? Here are five benchmarks of planning processes which I have experienced as bringing fresh perspective and energized thought to the groundwork of planning: 1) proactive planning, 2) a long-range view, 3) inviting of diversity, 4) building in reflection and 5) learning to be.

PROACTIVE PLANNING

If you are planning a garden in the winter months, nothing you can do will make summer come more quickly. You need to look ahead and assess when conditions will be right, how you are going to prepare the ground and which will be the most productive seeds to plant. It's the same with congregations. Proactive planning simply means the opposite of reactive planning. Instead of setting goals to deal with the problems that are presently pestering you, you build a plan based on a vision of what and who you want be as a congregation, even if you can't see the ground in which you will be planting this future.

Since a future vision of the congregation is the key to being able to plan proactively, it's a good idea to have the congregational formation piece already under your collective belt before you begin mapping out your plot. The ability to articulate who you think God is calling your congregation to be will determine the effectiveness of your efforts.

However, if you feel you need to add a strategizing element before a formation process is tackled (which may be the case in congregations suspicious of the time commitment or the subjective nature of formation), you can still do some planning which is proactive. Take a look at the latest vision statement your leadership group has produced (even if it is years old) and get the congregation to talk about its pros and cons. Take the insights of that conversation as the vision of the church on which you will base your proactive planning.

The point of proactive planning is to avoid a narrow focus. If you are looking at present problems like lack of resources and declining membership, your view will be restricted to outcomes you feel you have to achieve...like more money and people. As in my garden planning, you will look for success only in results which match the glossy pictures on seed packages. In the case of congregational development, those glossy pictures usually look like the exultant mega-churches with parking lots full of BMWs and pews full of successful young adults. You won't be able to appreciate anything that develops which doesn't fit that static picture.

Basing your plan to move into the future on a vision to which God is calling your particular congregation will get you out of a narrowly defined box of success. It provides more latitude for seeing progress and achievement. For example, if I had said, "This garden is for the delight of my body and soul" I would have been more ready to enjoy the arrival of my bunnies.

What if your congregation said, "We are called to be a vital welcoming congregation to all ages of people" instead of "We desperately need more people!"? With such a goal you could focus on exploring all the ways of being more open and inviting, without getting stuck on counting up the numbers in pews every Sunday. Maybe in the long run it will be your educational program on Wednesday nights that attracts people. Maybe your outreach program will make outcasts feel at home. Those are measures of success which need to be celebrated as fruitful partnership with God, no matter what financial gain or drain is experienced. If your vision of the value of the church is connected to your relationship with God, success will take on varied and surprising forms.

A LONG-RANGE VIEW

The real challenge to being proactive is to look past the present context with its pressing problems, to a future more than a year or two away. This can test the resolve of any group of people, especially if you are in a winter which seems never ending. But long range planning, looking ahead 10 or 20 years, is of utmost importance at this point in time when changes come at us so suddenly and dramatically.

One of our most enduring and, in this case, unhelpful qualities as an American people is our "can do" spirit, taking on any problem as a crisis to be solved right now. This often leads us to treat the symptoms of a much deeper problem as superficial wounds... or even misreading as a problem a trend which is really a healthy shift (or would be if left to develop).

In planning to learn, we don't ignore the fact that difficulties may need to be addressed right away. Instead, we concentrate on the fact that problems are temporary and development is ongoing. The plan we are creating must take us past the temporary context and setbacks we are now encountering, to discover where more fertile, more consistently productive fields lie or can be created.

What we are looking for with the long-range view are not detailed instructions on what to do, but the kind of general outline of the ministry and mission which you think you will be planting, and how you think these seeds might best be nourished. You will learn by your successes and your mistakes. Specifics can be modified as you go, while the general plan keeps the congregation focused and learning along the way.

INVITING OF DIVERSITY

I had in mind, when I first planted my little garden, that I would be open to learning which types of vegetables and herbs did best in the soil I created. What I didn't have in mind, and was at first unable to accept, was the intrusion of rabbits. It's my experience that congregations have similar blind spots. They work on being open to a particular group which seems different from them – say parents with young children. Then, with an ironic sense of humor, God sends them old homeless people. What to do?

When you plan for diversity, you plan to be surprised by God. Remember, the whole point of being Church is to be God's partner, (and a junior partner, at that). Therefore, treat every unexpected twist, bump and challenge to your plan as a possible modification by God. The fact is that none of us can see very far ahead into the future and that we often end up with something we didn't foresee or expect. With God's presence, those surprises can be positive.

The ability to adapt is a more useful skill to have than accurate foresight. When planning to learn, part of the challenge is to be ready for what you think will grow. Just as important, though, is to keep those plans general enough to be flexible no matter what happens. You put up tomato frames and then the snow didn't melt until June? Maybe peas will grow more quickly and they can use those frames too.

Here's an example of how inviting diversity might look in congregational planning. I was working with a Native American congregation once, when they identified that music was very important to them. The members of this church had grown up singing the old hymns of our denomination accompanied by an organ and a piano, both still sitting in the front of their little chapel. However, there was no current member who could play the keyboard, and no one could think of anyone who could help. Still, they longed for an organist who would accompany them and a choir director who could help them develop this ministry. We simply put "develop musically" as one of the goals for the future, with no idea how that would work out.

An organist did not show up. However, a student from a nearby town needed a place to stay. The congregation agreed to let him room in the unused rectory. It turns out he was a music major, studying voice. He began to worship with them and pretty soon he began to gather children around him to sing. This little choir began to perform for the congregation. They sang camp songs and simple contemporary praise tunes. The church was once again filled with music. It was not what they had wished for or expected. It was better! Not only did they have music, but they found a way to encourage young people to participate as well.

If this congregation had made it their goal to find an organist and to sing beloved traditional hymns, they would have failed. But because there was the wide open intention to develop musically, they recognized in a new person strange and unforeseen gifts that would nurture them all. They were on the watch for God's hand in their midst, so they were able to recognize a new form of an old and beloved ministry.

The little children's choir may be dissolved now, but the goal of developing musically can still be valid in that community. God may send another leader, or one of the members may recognize a call to a music ministry which had not been heard before. Years from now that goal may still be a part of this congregation's unfolding plan. This is the kind of adaptable planning which will generate success in whatever context the congregation finds itself.

BUILDING IN REFLECTION

If you plan with a long range view and openness to diversity, how can you know if you are indeed moving in the right direction or just avoiding challenges? How can you assess which, out of the many ministries that could be nurtured and encouraged, are those that will grow the healthiest, most faithful congregation possible? The answer is to fold in ongoing, unflinching reflection on the progress of your plan. This is where planning and learning meet most productively.

Reflection also goes by the name "evaluation". In the story of my garden, it might look something like this: I planted marigolds to help control insects and to delight my eyes with their beauty. In looking back over the summer, I assess that the bugs weren't bad at all. The flowers were indeed beautiful, until the rabbits ate them all. They were very hardy flowers, however, and came back in greater glory after they were demolished.

Did marigolds attract the rabbits? I don't think so, as the bunny family had established itself firmly before eating them. Did eating the flowers keep the rabbits from eating other things, like tomatoes and basil? Maybe... Overall, I think the marigolds were a good thing and will replant them next year. They were more helpful than not in fulfilling my goal to nourish my body and delight my soul.

In a congregation, reflection can take such a simple form. The key is to do it regularly and for every ministry, even those long-established and considered inviolate by the congregation. In

Community Organizing this simple discipline is taught for every component, every action that is taken: First, plan the action. Second, act (actually do what you have planned). Finally, evaluate. Ask the questions which will tell you whether and at what level you have been successful. (Some community organizers actually grade each action they take, so that they have a sense of how much improvement is needed.)

Such an evaluation may lead you to do things differently. However, it's important not to give up too quickly on goals and objectives. Sometimes it takes multiple tries for a ministry offering to take off. But if such reflection is practiced every time, you are committing to improving your effort with every incidence of it, learning as you go.

See p. 220 for a sample agenda for MMRs – Mutual Ministry Reviews

After a good amount of time, usually a year, a more comprehensive reflection of the whole ministry of the congregation should be undertaken. This is when not only new efforts, but also the traditional ministries must be held up to the light of the overall plan and evaluated for effectiveness. A helpful free guide to such annual and inclusive evaluations (often called Mutual Ministry Reviews or MMRs), is "Living into Our Ministries: The Mutual Ministry Cycle" [34]

When doing reflection, it's important to keep in mind two things: First of all, no particular action is sacred. For example, worship is central to most congregations, but the form of worship, if not nourishing the body and the partnership with God, can change. Again, Christian education is indeed a positive. But if no one is coming to class at the traditional Sunday morning time, adjustments need to be made. This can be very threatening to some members, so be sure to keep in front of yourselves the basics of your calling in relationship with God. That calling is sacred.

The second thing to remember is that actions which don't produce results central to the values of the community, wear people out. There will be less energy and enthusiasm for new endeavors, if people are sucked dry trying to do the things they have always done but which are not bearing fruit. Whenever there is grousing about being the only people to do any work around here, or when sign-up sheets for volunteers go untouched, suspect a worn-out effort.

The key to pruning ministerial efforts is to do reflection as a communal exercise. If a critical mass of members understand the need for evaluation of each ministry, and if they are involved in the decisions made, then the progress of the plan will be supported.

LEARNING TO BE

Planning to plant when you can't even see the ground can be a frightening prospect. We all like to think we can predict what is under the snow, what will happen in the future. The truth is, however, that if people were ever very good at such prognosis, they are not now. With the context of our lives changing in the areas of culture, communication, technology and politics at an exponential rate, even the best forecasters are being put out of business, and the process of planning is becoming even more challenging.

Given the impossibility of the task, Jesus' approach of spelling out how to be is essential. In the beatitudes, those bullet points of blessing which Jesus outlined in the Sermon on the Mount, we are given a direction, a sketchy map of how we are to BE, instead of concrete goals to get us there. Perhaps Jesus understood better than anyone else that you can't control the future. You can only meet the time ahead with both intention and an openness to embrace whatever context you find there.

We are empowered to meet the future with confidence and creativity when we cultivate the attitude that planning is really learning how to live out our being as God's beloved partners in any given context. The other benchmarks of a planning process (proactive, a long-range view, inviting of diversity and building in reflection) need to work in harmony with this quality of being in the community.

PROGRAMS FOR PLANNING AS LEARNING

The following programs are one which I have found helpful, not only in planning but in learning. You may have others which meet the criteria above. Keep in mind that many programs can be tweaked to provide the benchmarks above.

A CONGREGATIONAL RULE OF LIFE

St. Benedict was the first Christian monk who formed his community around a Rule of Life, i.e. a set of understandings which provided the benchmarks for living and being together. This ancient practice of spelling out how we are to be together and with God is very helpful when looking towards the future. It provides a framework for shaping annual goals, because it delineates the values and priorities the community must practice if it is to retain its identity.

Many other groups and individuals have found this kind of framework helpful for their spiritual learning and growth, from individuals to groups like Alcoholics Anonymous.

The communal formation program *Rooted in God* ends with a workshop designed to help the whole congregation craft a Rule of Life. During the formation program, members consider how the Benedictine values of Stability, Obedience and Transformation could be lived out in their modern church setting. Hours of conversation have revealed the special calling of the parish. At the Rule of Life workshop, participants in the formation program review these topics and their insights with the whole congregation. Then, an outline of how the congregation will approach life together is created.

For some Rule of Life examples, see p. 218

It's important to understand the definition of "rule" in a Rule of Life not as a law to be obeyed, but more like a ruler which allows you to assess progress, or a banister which gives you support as you climb a stair. This "rule" points a direction into the future. It creates a guideline for maturing and responding to the developing context of the community.

What is amazing to me is the variety of Rules that I have seen emerge from this workshop. Each community is unique in how it thinks about itself and how it organizes for ministry. If you have been doing the *Rooted in God* formation program, then creating a communal Rule of Life will make sense and flow out of your work together.

If you have not used *Rooted in God* as your formation piece, the workshop provided there will not be helpful. However, you might still want to use the theory of a "Rule of Life" and build your own way of inviting the congregation to create one. Keep in mind that such a process should identify the common values and priorities of the whole membership, which will take time to explore (especially if you have not yet done the communal formation piece). Those values and priorities can then be translated into the ministry themes which the whole group will support and pursue.

While writing a Rule of Life is proactive, takes the long view, and plans for diversity, it does not specifically address the need for ongoing reflection and revision. And because the emphasis here is on the areas which the community commits to develop together over the long run, annual goals also need to be set and evaluated at regular intervals. If you choose to use either the workshop or another way of writing a Rule of Life, the inclusion of an annual Mutual Ministry Review is recommended.

PROVOCATIVE PROPOSITIONS

Another way to organize the priorities and values that the congregation wishes to nourish moving into the future is to use provocative propositions. These statements are part of the Appreciative Inquiry process. If AI was the foundation of the communal formation program, it makes a lot of sense to follow through with planning in this mode.

Sue Hammond, in *The Thin Book of Appreciative Inquiry*, says: "The purpose of provocative propositions is to keep our best at a conscious level."[35] In other words, these statements are meant to express the group's way of being, more than prescriptions of exactly what to do. They are general proclamations about areas which the AI interview process discovered to be a valuable part of the life of the congregation. There is a general desire to carry these values and ministries forward, although the congregation recognizes that it might have to be in a different way.

A garden example of creating a provocative proposition might go something like this: I really liked the marigolds I planted in the past. I appreciated that they were pretty and that they had pest retardant properties. Therefore, a statement which will guide the future development of my garden might look like this: I incorporate both beauty and natural defenses into my garden plot.

A provocative proposition throws you into the future with your values intact, so that anything which happens in a new context can be dealt with by building not on a particular experience (such as marigolds) but on the treasured values (beauty and natural defenses). What happens if next year there is an epidemic which wipes out all marigolds, or I learn that growing marigolds was indeed what attracted the rabbits?

No problem. I simply go back to my values and find a different way to bring beauty and defenses to my little plot. Perhaps I will put in chrysanthemums this year, which are both pretty and unsavory to insects. And while I'm researching, I find that catnip may help discourage bugs too... with the additional benefit of keeping my cats happy!

The key to writing good provocative propositions is to "... apply 'what if' to all the common themes. Then write affirmative present tense statements incorporating the common themes."[36] In a congregational setting, you would look at all the common and positive themes which came up in AI interviews. If, as in our church example above, the congregation fondly remembers the organ and piano accompanying the members while they sang the old hymns, the theme of "music in church" would be identified as an important value.

Ask of that value, "What if?" What if there could be music in our church enriching worship all the time? What would we say of ourselves then? How about something like: We have a vibrant music ministry.

Such a statement may not be true in the sense that it is already happening. It is true in that it is the way this congregation wants to be. It is a central value which carries the challenge to the whole church. If this is who you want to be, how will you work on being that today and next year and the year after that?

I like provocative propositions a lot. They embody the spirit of a Rule of Life, while being even simpler to imagine and design. They are proactive, long range and inviting of diverse people and ministries as they are pursued.

The real drawback to provocative propositions is that, while creating them is fun and energizing, they provide no structure for follow-through. There is no strategy for setting goals to pursue these statements of value and no built-in method to reflect on how the congregation is doing as they work on them. It is tempting to create these statements, share them with the whole congregation, pat ourselves on the back and then forget all about them as the contingencies of life confront us. Be ready with a strategy for setting annual goals and consider the Mutual Ministry Review as a way to infuse more structure into this program.

If you like the format of provocative propositions, but have not been using Appreciative Inquiry (or not done the formation piece at all yet), you can still use the central values and priorities you have established to construct these types of statements. Be aware, though, that part of the power of the propositions is that people can see in them the answers they gave in their AI interviews. They identify with and support the values. That buy-in is central to the success of provocative propositions.

RESEARCH ACTIONS AND GENERAL ASSEMBLIES

The discipline of Community Organizing also offers tools for "planning as learning". If you are a larger church which is using Community Organizing tools for formation, this process may be your best choice.

Likely you have used both Relational Meetings and House Meetings to identify the values and priorities which your members are motivated to pursue. The CO tool of Research Action is the logical next step in planning to build on these areas of interest you have identified. While in the political sphere this step is often focused on one overall goal (i.e. the passing of legislation or getting a particular person elected), in congregational life it's more helpful to get several groups of leaders working on different topics which are of interest to the majority of members.

You may have identified several such areas in your initial meetings. Say the congregation seems motivated by issues of evangelism, increasing its outreach, and deepening its worship experiences. Those three topics can become the topics of Research Actions.

After establishing the broad themes of the Research Actions, the most important point to consider is the people you will invite to be part of these research teams. Hopefully, during your relational and house meetings you have identified the types of leaders in your midst. For Research Actions, you want to include at least one or two red or "primary" leaders (those who can see the big picture and help empower people to work together).

You also want the majority of the research group to be motivated around the chosen topic. So, yellow or "secondary" leaders (those who have a passion about a particular ministry, population or cause) should be invited, even if their focus is narrower than the presenting theme. For example, you may have a member who is passionate about including more youth in the congregation. Another member may be focused on welcoming the new Latino people in the neighborhood. Both of these members will have something to say about evangelism. We depend on the red leaders to help them see this and work together!

The most important thing about Research Actions is that they bring together people who are motivated around the same cause. Once you get them in the same room, the trick is to create an environment which will help them come up with a creative way to construct a strategic and learning centered plan in these areas. Armed with conversational skills and the freedom to come up with some truly innovative ways of addressing the future, the energy and enthusiasm of these groups can be amazing! Check out how these were structured in one church setting (p. 157) for some ideas of how to do your own.

Go to p. 157 for "Developing Church Leaders in a Neighborhood

When all the Research Action groups have come up with strategies to develop their particular areas, they present these plans to the whole congregation in a General Assembly. The main intent of this meeting is to vividly present the story of how these goals were created out of the congregation's DNA. A vision of how the church might pursue them together is then portrayed, along with extending an invitation to be part of the wonderful plans. All participants in the Research Action groups should be involved in this presentation. Specific tactics for inviting those members not yet involved should be in place. This is drama at its best, weaving stories of individuals and the congregation into the evolving story of the people of God.

The community organizing process of "planning as learning" involves a creative model using small groups. It is proactive and can take (if the research actions are well run) a long range view. The final plans will invite diversity as well, if the members of the research actions are open to each other's ideas and represent a broad spectrum of the congregation.

The weakness in this model, like the others mentioned, is that a process for reflection is left to theory. A specific model of annual reflection is not built into this process to ensure that learning will continue throughout the years ahead. The addition of some kind of Mutual Ministry Review is recommended.

SCENARIO PLANNING

Scenario Planning is another process for "planning to learn" as the future is addressed. Scenarios, while not predicting the outcomes of the world and our place in it, allow us to think about the changing context of the world in many varied and creative ways. Investing time in learning this technique, (or money in hiring a consultant who will walk your congregation through it), would be helpful for most congregations and, indeed, the wider Church.

While the process is too complicated in to go into here, a bare outline may be helpful as you consider options. The Scenario Planning process is based on the idea that the future is moving towards us too quickly to predict. The best we can do is to identify which factors will impact our situation the most and then imagine the possibilities which may develop in those areas. These issues may vary from something as big as global warming to as close to home as whether your denominational office will continue funding congregations.

After sorting out which of these critical factors will affect your congregation most, scenarios are written by small teams. Scenarios are simply stories about your community written in the future tense from an imagined period of time some 15 to 20 years ahead. The writers try to imagine how the world will look if the critical factors develop in different ways, and how your congregation might respond.

The stories are shared with the whole planning group and patterns are noticed. What factors don't seem to change much in each of the imagined futures? Which futures depend on factors which develop in dramatically different ways? Would any single action be positive in all the imagined scenarios? If not, which one would be the safest? Which would bring the greatest benefits if the congregation bet on it and that particular future came true?

Questions like these open up the conversation and keep it proactive, long range and envisioning diversity. Evaluation is built in as the planning group continues to check at regular intervals to see if the world seems more on track with one scenario than another... or if events point to an entirely different eventuality.

The Art of the Longview by Peter Schwartz contains a wonderful description of how to create and use stories of the future as the basis of strategic planning.[37] While scenario planning was developed as a business approach to strategic planning, if you have done your formation work and have the foundational awareness of God's call to lead you, the process can be exciting and energizing to the congregation. It covers all the benchmarks of a good "planning as learning" process. Members of a planning group will have only to suffuse the process with the moral compass of their relationship with God.

PLANNING AS SURVIVAL

"We understand that the only competitive advantage the company of the future will have is its ability to learn faster than their competitors."[38]

This quote is from a businessman, but it seems to me that it's important for us in the Church to take his insight seriously. We may not like to think of ourselves as competitors, but we need to survive in a world of competing interests, of developing needs and wants which consume the creation of God. How we learn to cope will determine if the love of God will continue shine forth through the Church.

Some days I think the challenge of being Church in the future is like being sent to Mars as the very first gardeners in outer space. We know what is needed to grow food and flowers on Earth: seeds, soil, sun and water. But how do we provide those necessities in such a wildly different setting? Shall we build giant greenhouses in an attempt to recreate the attributes of Earth? Is there a possibility that with a little tweaking we could actually grow plants in the soil of Mars? Are there varieties of plants that would thrive under such conditions? What do we need to learn BEFORE the spaceship takes off and we are irretrievably stuck in that new atmosphere?

The fact is that God's children will need to be fed on Mars. The fact is that even on Earth they will need to be fed, in the next twenty years, whether we face the challenge or not. It is a tremendous and scary responsibility.

Our only hope is that we are not alone. We have a gardening partnership with God. God knows what creation needs, and will provide seed, sun, and the imagination to grow it. In fact, our most difficult challenge has to do with giving up ingrained assumptions, stripping down to the most basic of relationships with God, so that we can truly be for God. Then, and only then, will the Church survive. Then, and only then, will we be able to sing the Lord's song in the new land of the future and be blessed indeed.

CHAPTER 6 — CONVERSATION STARTERS

As your group begins to discuss, "A Plan to Learn", remember that this is only a part of the Congregational Development process. While planning is the jumping off point for many development projects, other elements have been suggested in this book which, if added to your soil before the planning ingredient, will help to make your effort on this front more productive. Consider carefully all the elements of development and when "planning to learn" should be added to the mix.

1) Reflect on what assumptions you hold, individually and as a group, about the future of your congregation 20 years in the future. What if these assumptions are true? What if they are false?

2) Dream together about how you want to be as a congregation in 20 years. What will people notice about the church and ministries? Try to discern what values are behind that dream.

3) Learning to be, and the flexibility of action that it implies, are central to this ingredient of development. If you were simply to describe your congregation's future in terms of being, what would that sound or look like?

4) Of the benchmarks (proactive planning, long-range view, inviting of diversity, building in reflection and learning to be), which will be the easiest for your congregation to embrace? Which the most difficult? Why?

5) Considering the suggested programs for "Planning to Learn" (and any others that you might be aware of), which of these fit your congregation? What will it take to initiate such a planning effort?

6) How will your planning group address any missing elements which a program needs to fit the benchmarks given? Are short-term goals included as well as the long view? Is the annual evaluation built in? If not, how will you plan for this?

CHAPTER 7

GIFTS AND NEEDS DISCERNMENT

"For as with the human body which is a unity although it has many parts-all the parts of the body, though many, still making up one single body-so it is with Christ. We were baptized into one body in a single Spirit, Jews as well as Greeks, slaves as well as free men, and we were all given the same Spirit to drink. And indeed the body consists not of one member but of many....Now Christ's body is yourselves, each of you with a part to play in the whole.

(I Corinthians 12:12-14, 27, The New Jerusalem Bible)

By midsummer, my tomatoes were looking pretty grim. It had been a late, snowy spring. I finally was able to put the plants in the ground the first week in June. By July they were still not producing much. I figured I had to do something to inspire them to put forth flowers and fruit. I had in mind simply buying a bag of fertilizer and quickly working it into the soil around the plants. A friend suggested a name brand, so I dutifully went to the nursery and looked for it specifically.

The recommended fertilizer came in a canister. When I shook some out, it looked like miniature bath beads. Luckily, I am an obsessive label reader and carefully perused the instructions before I began. Turns out, there was more to do than just dumping it on the ground. This potent stuff had to be applied in a very particular way in order not only to help the plants, but to keep from burning them as well.

Instead of just tossing these little beads in the dirt, I was instructed to 1) measure the amount I put on carefully, 2) make sure it was a certain distance from the stems of the plants, 3) water it right away after application and then 4) reapply in a month. This was more complicated than I had expected! It did produce results, but I'm sure I would have killed those plants if I had simply assumed this product was the same as other fertilizer.

FERTILIZING THE CONGREGATION

At the heart of Mutual Ministry is the belief that all members, ordained or not, are gifted and called to ministry. This is a given. But the discovery of what people are skilled at doing, want to do and how that will fit into the ministry of the church is an ingredient which needs to be added to the congregational garden plot very carefully.

It is easy to burn rather than nurture a church with this element. People can be placed in roles which are obviously not suitable for them, or they agree to a ministry and then don't follow through. There are tasks which no one will happily agree to take on. Sometimes congregation members find their discernment efforts have left them irritated, disappointed with each other and worse off than before. Why? Is this proof that Mutual Ministry is just not viable in the average congregation?

I think that sharing ministry is possible and that the depth of ministry in even the smallest of our churches can be astounding, but only if discernment is done well. The problem is that, like my efforts to fertilize tomatoes, we come to this element of congregational development with the assumption that we know what we are doing. We have what Peter Senge calls a mental model, i.e. "…deeply ingrained assumptions, generalizations or even pictures or images that influence the world and how we take action."[39] Our image of discernment blinds us to some important realities about this complex ingredient of church life.

ASSUMPTIONS ABOUT DISCERNMENT

In their work, *The Thin Book of Naming Elephants,* Hammond and Mayfield suggest that assumptions can be challenged by asking two questions: What if this is true? And what if this is false?[40] The following are two assumptions I find congregations often make around the ingredient of discernment. Uncovering and questioning these mental models will lead to new ways of thinking about the important element of discernment and, hopefully, a more successful way of applying it.

1ST ASSUMPTION

The first and foremost assumption made about discernment in the congregation is that church members are volunteers who will be doing volunteer tasks.

If this assumption is true, there will be a divide between paid staff and unpaid workers. "Volunteers" will always be second class ministers. Money is such a primary criterion for importance in our society. Even if these volunteer jobs include goals that have been set by a communal visioning process, we will look at them as lesser ministries, not worth the time of paid staff.

If the assumption that we are discerning for volunteer jobs is not true, we have to replace our mental model of expecting a group of volunteers to "help" a professional (or a group of professionals). What might that new model look like?

In congregations which can no longer afford to pay a professional rector/pastor, one gift poverty has given is the discovery of ministry teams. Where these teams are most successful, they are groups of radical equality. Members minister out of a profound sense of interdependence, challenging assumptions about hierarchical values. They go back to Paul's metaphor of the body and share his understanding that the eye and the hand, the butt and the brain all need each other to function.

In congregations which have a rector/pastor and other paid staff, can this mental model of interdependent equality supplant the assumption of the divide between professionals and volunteers? There is every reason to believe it can, if the community as a whole will agree to practice a different way of being together. A common understanding, a new mental model, must be applied.

One way to embrace this new model is to blend together the definition of professional and amateur. While a professional is understood by our culture as one who has more expertise than an amateur, its root word "profess" comes from the Latin, "to declare publicly". In monasteries, monks and nuns "profess" their belief and their commitment to live out their relationship with God. None of them are expert at this. They simply make it the focus of their lives and practice it together. They are, in a very real sense of the word, professional Christians.

The word "amateur" comes from the root word for love, indicating someone who does their work solely for the love of it. We often see this as "unprofessional" because of that pervasive cultural value we place on money. However, if professionals don't love what they are doing, especially in the context of serving in the Church, they will not be very good at it. Neither the work nor God will be served from their hearts.

Therefore, the mental model we want to create and adopt for this important ingredient of discernment is one where all members are equal ministers. They are all professionals, having professed that they are committed to do the work they are called to by virtue of their relationship with God. And they are also all amateurs, by virtue of throwing their heart into this work which they do for love of God.

When this new mental model is embraced by the congregation, discernment becomes just as important for unsalaried positions as salaried, because the central criterion is not money, but the commitment of one's life to partnership with God. In fact, there must be an effort made to be sure that, even if they are paid, the salaried ministers are not forced into doing what they do not love…just to put bread on the table. To work at something one does not feel called to and which the community does not recognize as your gift is sacrilege in this model.

(This will be good news to many church "professionals" who struggle to do expected tasks 80% of the time, just to get to the 20% of the job they love!)

2ND ASSUMPTION

The second assumption congregations often make is that simply naming someone's gifts and skills will automatically release those gifts for ministry in the congregation.

If this were true, than discernment would indeed be an easy element to fold into any congregational garden. All we would need to do is set aside a Saturday to do a workshop with those clever spiritual gifts inventories, score them, enter the data into the church computer and, voila! 100% participation by everyone!

However, in my experience, there are a number of problems with this assumption. I have not found a level of organization in most church offices which is needed for the ongoing coordination of identified gifts with needed jobs. Furthermore, both ministries and ministers are continually evolving. This makes such match-ups a moving target, requiring a more organic than mechanistic approach.

Another issue is that simple inventories usually ignore components such as undeveloped skills, motivations and leadership qualities. Remember that many of the heroes of the Bible, (like Moses, Mary, and Paul), would never have been discerned as central players had they been judged by skill sets or prior experience. An element of motivation, of mystery and of divine intervention has to be allowed for. The movement of the Holy Spirit must be taken into account. The work of discernment can be messy and confusing, asking us to risk rather than play it safe.

So, given the above, what if the assumption that just naming peoples' gifts will release them for ministry is false? Well, then you have a lot of disappointed people who have been promised that they will be valued and used to do God's work, sitting around feeling unwanted. If the church never calls on them to do anything, (or worse, calls them to do what is not life-giving), we are back at square one. It's also discouraging for congregations to realize that "gifts discernment" is not a silver bullet solution to their labor shortage and finance problems.

It seems as if a new mental model is necessary for how we think about releasing gifts for ministry. I suggest that we replace the assumption of the ease of transforming knowledge of gifts into active ministry with the understanding that discernment will be an ongoing, in-depth process of getting to know ourselves and each other, as God sees us. This new way of thinking means that we have to listen very closely to subjective opinions, trying to put together the truth of each person's calling by comparing different viewpoints. We have to be willing to take risks, make mistakes, and start over (without shaming or shunning participants). Such a mental model must also carefully monitor members as they mature in their ministries and in their relationship to God, taking those developments into consideration, as well.

These two new mental models take the discernment of gifts to a whole different level in the life of a congregation. We give up the assumption of "professional vs. volunteer" ministries for commitment to a ministry team made up of professional amateurs (or amateur professionals). We leave behind the delusion that simply naming the talents people have somehow releases them for ministry, and embrace the understanding that ministry develops most fully out of honest and loving relationships. Discernment and calling for ministry becomes a central effort of our life together. We can now take this element seriously and apply the steps for discernment in a way that will nourish the congregation.

STEPS FOR APPLYING DISCERNMENT

There are four steps to be addressed in the application of this ingredient: 1) Discerning the gifts of the members, 2) Discerning ministries, 3) The calling and 4) Training and education. Because all four are required for discernment to be effective and not harmful to the congregation, I will suggest some programming for each separate component of this element.

STEP 1 — DISCERNING THE GIFTS OF THE MEMBERS

The first step of applying discernment is actually paying attention to the people of the congregation. In small churches especially, members may think that, of course, they know what the gifts and calling of each member is. After all, these people have been doing their thing in church for most of their lives. But assumptions on this level are as dangerous as those on a larger stage. To approach seeing another person as God sees them, we need to find a way to articulate both the self-knowledge people have and the perceptions of those who know and love them, while leaving room for unexpected revelations.

In this step, several areas require attention. The initial focus is usually on spiritual gifts, skills and talents. These are manifest in a person's life and history, gleaned from what a person is known to have accomplished. While many people have a sense of who they are in this way, I have also been surprised at how difficult it is for individuals to name positive aspects about themselves. Often they need the affirmation of their neighbors to be able to claim their obvious gifts.

As well as those manifest talents and skills, the undeveloped gifts of a person need to be surfaced and considered for development. I have found that uncovering a person's motivation (i.e. why they are engaged in particular actions) often will lead us to ask: Could a deeper gift be hidden here that is just crying to be unleashed? Is there a dream which has never been nurtured in this person that the congregation could support?

An example of this is a woman from a small town who was identified by others as a potential church leader. I developed a relationship with her and asked her to participate in several inter-church activities, which she was glad to do. Then one day she called to ask if she could accompany me to the Reservation and support my work with a Native American congregation. No one had noticed her desire to work with a different culture. I'm not sure she was even aware of it herself until she heard what I was doing. I was at first skeptical that this blonde blue-eyed young woman was really called to be part of a Native American ministry. Both she and I took the leap. Now, years later when my path has led me away, this woman is still faithfully and effectively ministering with that congregation.

Skills, talents and spiritual gifts (both those exercised and those undeveloped), emerge for ministry through the efforts of the whole community. The use of inventories could be a beginning point, if whatever these tests reveal is not taken as absolute and is followed up by discussion among members to affirm and more deeply explore members' strengths. If your congregation wants to use such a tool, I would recommend the one found in Christian Schwartz's book, *The Three Colors of Ministry*.[41] While the language may present a barrier to more mainline denominations (it's rather evangelical) this is the only inventory I know which asks two other people to share their perceptions of the test taker. It also indicates "latent" gifts, or areas which the person might want to explore for development.

Go to p. 223 for the
Gifts Discernment

I think that while such inventories may start a conversation about gifts, they also feed into the assumption that it is easy to know and peg people for ministry. I am much more comfortable with beginning a dialogue about gifts in a small group setting. This environment encourages people to share what they know about themselves and then, through guided conversation, receive feedback from others who know them. Over the years, I have developed a gifts discernment workshop, adding to it the option of identifying motivations as well as known skills, which you might find helpful.

It's not enough to simply identify gifts. It's also important to be aware of the style and quality of leadership that members exercise, if at all possible. Calling a person to be in charge of coordinating others on a ministry project can be colossal failure, if the person is an "I'll do it myself" kind of leader. If there is a need to bridge differing viewpoints in a program and the person called to lead has energy for only one aspect of the work, other team members will be discouraged or angered.

Conversely, calling someone who is capable of bringing people together and empowering them, to perform only single, solitary tasks, is a sure way to lose ministers to secular opportunities which honor their abilities.

Our new mental model of radical equality in ministry rejects the understanding of a leader as one who forges ahead on their own, leaving others to follow. Embracing that new model, community organizing defines leaders as anyone who can bring another person to the table. In Community Organizing, the table is where visioning is shared and negotiation happens. In the Church, the meaning of bringing people to the table expands to include inviting them into relationship (and ultimately partnership) with God.

If the CO definition of leader is accepted by the congregation, then they will understand that, just as everyone is a minister, everyone is also at times a leader. But people bring others to the table in very different ways. Here again Community Organizing is helpful in providing a template for those different leadership styles.

Go to p. 166 for more info on CO leadership

For work in a congregational community, I have modified the instruction I received on leadership personalities (from training in the Industrial Areas Foundation method of Community Organizing).

Very briefly, the types of leaders include:

1) Red leaders who are relational "bridge builders" and most interested in empowering everyone
2) Yellow leaders who focus on a particular issue or population
3) Blue leaders who, out of a personal skill or gift, attract other individuals

Simply being aware of these types of leaders (and combinations of them) can help members understand how they might be most effective in ministry. Exploring these definitions, and making leadership a quality to be included in discernment conversations is important. If everyone is aware of differences and (mindful of Paul's metaphor of the body) values these different styles, the leadership factor can readily be folded into a gifts discernment process.

It is most important to remember that discernment around the gifts, skills, motivations and leadership styles of members is not a one-shot deal. As my fancy fertilizer directions insisted: "Repeat in one month!" Maybe a month will be too early for the whole congregation to make another concerted effort…but a yearly check-in with how people are seeing their ministry developing at the time of a Mutual Ministry Review is certainly appropriate.

And it's imperative for the topic of discernment to surface regularly in the conversations of members as the work of the congregation is planned and carried out. Instead of just tagging the same people to do the same things over and over again ask, "Who do we now know has the capabilities and motivation for this ministry?" Another good question to keep on top of the table is "Who could we be mentoring, so they can eventually step into these ministries?"

If discernment is part of ongoing conscious dialogue in the congregation, it will also facilitate folding new members into ministries for which they are fit. Newcomers don't take root until they have a sense of belonging. Their first need is for relationship. Connecting with them and befriending them is the most positive thing we can do for those who come in the front door. And while members are "befriending" these potential congregants, they can be listening hard for what motivates these new people, what skills they bring, and what kind of leaders they might be.

Obviously, in this mental model, gifts discernment is not a week-end workshop job. It is about encouraging members, old and new, to continue being curious about each other. It is about looking closely for where God is working in our lives and the lives of others in our congregation. It is, ultimately and at the root, about relationship. That is where the minister is truly discerned and called forth.

STEP 2 — DISCERNING MINISTRIES

While the gifts of members are being discerned, ministries appropriate to the congregation's call also need to be under consideration.

Some people say that anything and everything done by Christians is ministry. I think they may be right…in the sense that Brother Lawrence was right when he encouraged people to make everything they did, from scrubbing the floors to saying prayers, an offering to God.[42] However, for our purposes, we want to focus in on the call of the congregation, and the ministries which must be done to develop the church in that particular direction.

If you have already developed goals for your congregation, now is the time to get them out and take a look at them. If you haven't, get out your long-range plan and make some yearly goals. If you haven't done either... this will be a hard step for you to do. At the very least, see where your congregation wants to develop and grow.

Form a group of people to articulate what ministries are needed to pursue those goals. In some congregations, your development team may take this on. Others may want the vestry, session or other established board included. Often, members already participating in the general area or even the specific ministry will be asked to lend their expertise.

The work of spelling out exactly what kind of ministry is being asked for and what is needed to get it done, can be tedious and time consuming. Almost every congregation I have worked with has wanted to skip, or at least curtail, this task. Bad idea! Not being specific about the definition and scope of a ministry has led to many a member and congregation being burned by bad calls. You may think that everyone knows what it takes to teach Sunday school, start an outreach ministry or participate on the altar guild. They don't. Assumptions abound and lead to much misunderstanding and pain.

On the other hand, if you put effort into articulating definitions of the needed ministries, you have a double advantage. First, you are making more appropriate calls. Secondly, you gain the whole congregation's understanding of those ministries. This will pay off down the road, as people work together with a deeper appreciation of their interdependence.

For a sample Ministry Role Description, go to p.

The most organized way to define ministries is by writing ministry role descriptions. There are forms available for such an effort. If you are already using *The Three Colors of Ministry*, you can access a very comprehensive one in the back of this book.[43]

Otherwise, just make up a uniform list of questions to be answered about each ministry being considered, which can be addressed by those job descriptions.

These questions should include the following:

a) ***What is the goal of this ministry?***
   The task or role is described by setting forth the primary goal and any other secondary objectives to the task. For example, perhaps one of the ministry roles which your congregation wants to pursue is that of "Welcome Team Leader". The primary goal of this ministry may be to form a team of members who will be trained and mobilized to welcome people into the life of the congregation. Secondary goals

may be to keep the congregation informed about events and developments with potential members and to inform the governing body of any financial and scheduling support that is needed.

Note here – you don't want to describe the role too closely, or even become too wed to these goals. The person or persons called to do this, if they are creative and inspired, may take the ministry in a direction which no one else has anticipated. But, because expectations have been laid out to begin with, there is a foundation from which to build and a way to dialogue if expectations change.

b) *Who will this minister work with (directly and indirectly) and who will support her/him?*

It is very important for the person called to a ministry role to be aware that they are not going to just be handed a task and left to figure it out by themselves. Think about what groups or individuals may provide support for this minister. In the case of a person responsible for gathering and directing other ministers, you might want to have a regular meeting of similar team leaders. Or perhaps you have a vestry/session/board which is responsible for oversight of ministry in the church, to which this person could regularly report and share.

c) *What gifts, skills, talents and leadership qualities do we think would be most helpful to this ministry?*

This is where the writers fantasize about what qualities they think would best equip a person for this job. In the case of the "Welcome Team Leader, they might answer: This person will succeed most readily if they are a red leader, able to bring different people together and empower them. This minister should have a heart for the stranger and a gift for hospitality. Creativity and innovation will be a plus as will the ability to communicate well with the group.

There is no need for very detailed descriptions of gifts and talents. The real trick is to be able to recognize that the member actually called to this position may have only a few of these gifts. The description is simply something to shoot for, trusting the Holy Spirit to move us towards members with the right potential.

d) *What are the time expectations of this ministry?*

There are two issues to be considered with time expectations. The first is how many hours per week (or per month) are required for this role? Are there any specific hours which must be kept? It's important to give an estimate of time required so that members can make responsible decisions about accepting calls.

The writers of the "Welcome Team Leader" role description may estimate that the position will take about six hours a month. They expect this minister will call one monthly meeting plus spend an hour a week on the phone or writing articles. They also feel that this minister should attend Sunday services regularly, so that he or she will have first-hand knowledge of how new comers are greeted, and can make announcements for this ministry. While expectations are negotiable, they are put in the description so assumptions are up front and on the table.

The other time issue which needs to be articulated is the duration of the commitment. It's my experience that congregations rarely look ahead to ending the calls they have extended. However, to expect a Sunday school teacher or a soup kitchen director to have a lifelong commitment to those tasks is a bit much. Failing to provide for graceful exits from jobs which no longer excite and nurture members can lead to burn out or, even worse, rust out from boredom.

A clear period of time which the person is expected to remain in this job does not mean that they have to leave when the time is up. It simply marks a point when evaluation of the ministry will be done. If the ministry fit is a good one and nourishing to both minster and congregation, the call may be renewed.

What is an appropriate time period for the duration of a ministry commitment? Usually a few years is reasonable, with evaluations scheduled at the time of the congregation's Mutual Ministry Review. However, if there is a long mentoring or training period, a longer commitment could be expected. And of course, ordained positions in some denominations are for life (although the focus of ministry in such roles may shift with time and experience).

e) *What education and training are needed?*

No one likes to be taken by surprise by requirements which pop up after a commitment has been made. As much as possible, the writers of these role descriptions should anticipate denominational expectations, as well as the congregation's sense of what training is needed for a particular ministry. Opportunities for education and training need to be listed. If money is tight and training opportunities are rare, a period of mentoring may do just as well or better.

Record the answers to the above five questions for each of the ministries for which the congregation will be discerning ministers. These documents, circulated so everyone has a chance to be familiar with them, become the backbone of your calling process, which is the next step in the discernment application process.

STEP 3 — THE CALLING

Ideally, every member now has a list of their own gifts and skills, as well as a sense of their leadership style and motivation. Ideally, every ministry role which is open for a new participant has been described and expectations explained. Now you are ready for the congregation to issue calls.

If you fall short of this ideal, don't worry. Like gardening, calling is an imprecise activity and allows for a lot of leeway. Eventually you just have to dive into the process, knowing that it is ongoing and you can pick up the people and ministries you missed on another round.

The most important point to hold onto here is that "calling" is the function of the whole congregation, not just the clergy or a small discernment group. The church as a whole needs to take a look at where each member will function in this body of Christ. But how to do it?

Eventually, I think calling will become second nature to congregations. People will know each other and themselves so well that the natural fit between minister and ministry will slide smoothly into place. But while we are in the process of adjusting to new mental models which challenge us with radical equality and a long term approach to discernment, I think the process is helped by a little structure and imposed focus.

Go to p. 230 for the Congregational Calling Workshop

Not finding a program which covered the bases of structure and focus, I developed "The Congregational Calling Workshop". The goal of this exercise is to create an environment which centers members on listening to God. In this setting, participants float the skills, gifts and leadership styles which they have discovered about themselves and others, alongside the descriptions of the congregation's desired ministries. The result is a group discernment which surfaces names for each ministry role. Individuals are then asked to consider committing to the particular ministries to which they have been named.

While I won't go into the workshop in detail here, I do want to mention criteria for a congregational calling process which will fit the bill. They are:

1) Information on both people and ministries is clear and shared with all
2) Members, through conversation and prayer, make lists of possible match ups between individuals and ministry roles
3) People are invited to consider the callings which the congregation has proposed and to respond
4) The process is completed within a set amount of time (two weeks seems sufficient in most cases) and the calls which have been accepted are made public.

I do want to note here that the individual's perception of his or her call must be honored. There are three answers a person can give to a congregational call: 1) Yes, 2) No, and 3) I'm not sure. The first two answers require simple acceptance from other members. The third uncertain answer provides an opportunity for other members to talk and pray with the person until clarity is reached.

An important recommendation in this calling process is advocating a limit of three roles to which each member may assent. Indeed, some may want to consider just one or two. In every congregation there are members who over-function (usually out of a generosity of heart). The truth is, though, that one member's busyness may deny those people who are less proficient or not as central to the congregation a chance to participate. Don't be afraid to let a ministry role lie fallow until the person God is calling comes to that conclusion as well.

In the case of ministry roles which require ordination, another layer of discernment by the wider church is often involved. Depending on your denomination, you may want to handle these callings in a more discreet manner, especially if you are required to receive judicatory leaders' permission before exploring the call with an individual. As denominations vary so widely on these matters, I would suggest contacting your judicatory representative before you go forward with calling for ordained roles.

Even though extra requirements may make the task of calling ordained leadership more difficult, I want to stress the positives such an effort brings. Clergy who have been called by the congregation they serve have a better chance of accepting a limited role on the ministry team. They won't expect to be the only "professional" Christians. If they are fortunate enough to be allowed to study for orders at home with their ministry team, they can avoid false assumptions of having secret knowledge and can continue to work together with the congregation in the radical equality which is necessary for Mutual Ministry to come to fruition. If your denomination is open to your congregation discerning members to the ordained ministry, this will facilitate your development immeasurably.

> ### STEP 4 — TRAINING AND EDUCATION

One of the instructions for applying that fancy fertilizer to my tomatoes was to water it right away and to water it well. Training and education constitute a similar step. You can identify the members' gifts, define the ministries, and get the calls right, but if you don't soak new ministers well with the necessary knowledge and skills to do their work, hoped for vocations never take off.

Here are some issues to consider when taking this last step in the application of discernment:

1) First, the congregation has financial responsibility for getting members what they need to succeed. Having called them to positions of equal ministry, a commitment to equipping them for those positions is implicit. In some cases this may take financial resources, or help in finding money, for classes, travel etc. (This is not to say an individual shouldn't pay part of their way, but the expectation should be that this gift is not required. Otherwise we need to be up front that we expect only people with discretionary cash to apply!)

   More than finances, emotional and spiritual support may be needed. In the best of situations, members will be taking on ministry roles which stretch and challenge them. An environment which provides timely and honest feedback, along with a communal commitment to help people do their best, must be cultivated. We'll explore this further in the next chapter, but it will be important for members to know that they have the prayers and active support of the whole congregation as they embark on new endeavors.

2) Secondly, although some roles may require specialized training, all ministries require ministers who have at least a foundational knowledge and expression of Christianity. The ability to articulate one's faith helps members become deeply rooted in their partnership with God. In the past, we depended on the priest or pastor to have the answers to all things theological and Christian. Non-ordained members were expected to be content to simply go along (or at least not make waves). That no longer works in a model of equal and interdependent ministries.

Everyone has a relationship with God and therefore a theology, whether conscious or not. The role of Christian education is not so much to tell people <u>what</u> to think as <u>how</u> to think about this relationship. Two excellent programs which invite learning at this level are *Education for Ministry*[44] and *LifeCycles*[45]. You may have other favorites. A strong adult Christian education program available to as many members as possible is of paramount importance to the success of shared ministry.

3) Finally, learning in groups of members is the preferred format for all education. In our new mental model which includes the radical equality of ministers, a barrier is raised when we assume that diplomas indicate wisdom. They don't. At most they prove that someone has had the discipline to study a particular subject for a set amount of time and satisfied the people in charge that they absorbed at least a nominal amount of the offered information.

To overcome this barrier, it's helpful to take a team approach to learning. If a member needs to be sent off to get certification for a specialized ministry, such as worship leader for example, it's important that he or she not go alone. In classes which focus on preparation for ordination, group participation is especially important. Having a learning buddy or two, even if that buddy is not called to the same role, will democratize education. If two or three people take the same course, there can be no presumption or assumption of "secret" knowledge.

Group learning also ensures that there is a broader interpretation of the material offered. It avoids the danger of one person's lens becoming the only valid one, while encouraging the kind of dialogue which is the foundation of true community. Members who study together tend to learn more as they bounce ideas off each other, and the whole congregation profits.

You may have to get creative with this, especially if your judicatory insists on sending people to seminary or week-end institutes to be trained. If this is the case, consider having the student put together a home study group who will read what is assigned and converse regularly about the material. I used such a small group of interested members to compliment my efforts when studying for my doctoral degree. I found my learning greatly enriched, and it was wonderful to see my congregational colleagues applying insights to their ministries in our church.

Study groups are also helpful if on-line courses are being taken. While people may use their home computers to attend the virtual classes, face-to-face dialogue with other members who are taking the class can give a depth to the course that most web seminars lack. Indeed, some institutions are now recommending this as the norm for online students.

The bottom line is, a little watering after the application of fertilizer goes a long way to carrying that nourishment to the roots and encouraging growth and fruition. A little care in providing the necessary training and education after the application of the calling process carries the true conviction to all that they are valued and indispensible ministers in the body of Christ.

FOLLOWING DIRECTIONS

I don't usually suggest following directions too closely when working with congregations. I rarely follow them myself. In the application of discernment however, care needs to be taken to adhere to all the steps above as much as possible. This is the trickiest ingredient to add to our garden plots. It depends on mental models, those basic shared assumptions, being in alignment with a vision of mutual, shared ministry.

It is hard work. The whole congregation must be involved. You must take the time needed to execute the entire process well...and then continue to carry through again and again until discernment is part of your congregation's culture. Why do this hard work?

Why? Because the greatest, deepest joy of our lives is to become who God calls us to be. We do not accomplish this by praying alone in a chapel. We become the people we are created to be by testing out our abilities and following God's will, supported and directed by others who are also committed to Christ.

Why? Because the fruits of ministry done by people called and empowered to be God's partners are creativity and energy. The assumption that discernment will solve the problems of the church may not be true in a silver-bullet, easy-fix sort of way, but it is nonetheless true in a deeper sense. Discernment applied equally, well and often is the cure for much of what ails our poor institution. This element has the capacity to create an environment for evolution in the Church, as people who profess to love the Lord take full ownership of their partnership with God and each other. There are no financial or labor shortages which can stop this movement once it gets going.

Why? Because the abundance of power in the Church exists not in its buildings, nor in its ordained leaders. It resides in the deep reserves of gifts that have been bestowed on all God's people. The key to releasing that treasure trove is in this complex element of discernment.

Be careful what you ask for: If you do indeed want your congregation to flower and bear fruit, follow the application steps and call forth the ministers of your congregation. Just know that you may have no idea of the bounty which will be unleashed. You may in fact be able to delight and feed the world!

CHAPTER 7 — CONVERSATION STARTERS

There is a lot to talk about when considering a discernment process! Planning for this element needs to be fairly comprehensive.

1) Fredrick Buechner said "The place God calls you to is the place where your deep gladness and the world's deep hunger meet."[46] What did he mean? What do you believe about being called?

2) What mental models does my congregation have about discernment? If they are not helpful to the Mutual Ministry vision, how might they be challenged and changed?

3) Of the total number of people in our congregation, what percentage view themselves as ministers? How might we broaden that percentage, if necessary?

4) Do you have role descriptions for any of the ministries being done in the congregation? Who might have a talent for organizing and facilitating the writing of these descriptions?

5) In terms of fitting the right people into the right ministries, our congregation's experience of that has been:

a- good
b- bad
c- mixed

What went right or wrong? How might we address the weaknesses and build on the strengths?

6) What Christian education programs are you now involved in? How has it effected the participants' articulation of their relationship with God? In terms of evangelism, how this could be helpful?

7) What is your experience of learning in groups?

CHAPTER 8

SYSTEMIC REORGANIZATION

"(God's Kingdom is like)...a man going off on an extended trip. He called his servants together and delegated responsibilities. To one he gave five thousand dollars, to another two thousand, to a third one thousand, depending on their abilities...

After a long absence, the master of those three servants came back and settled up with them. The one given five thousand showed him how he had doubled his investment. His master commended him: 'Good work! You did your job well. From now on be my partner.'

The servant with the two thousand showed how he also had doubled his master's investment. His master commended him: "Good work! You did your job well. From now on be my partner.'

The servant given the one thousand said, "...I was afraid I might disappoint you, so I found a good hiding place and secured your money. Here it is, safe and sound down to the last cent."

The Master was furious. 'That's a terrible way to live! If you knew I was after the best, why did you do less than the least? The least you could have done would have been to invest the sum with the bankers, where at least I would have gotten a little interest.

Take the thousand and give it to the one who risked the most. And get rid of this "play-it-safe" who won't go out on a limb. Throw him out into utter darkness." (Matt. 25: 14-30, from The Message[47])

This is what I notice about myself when it comes to an endeavor I'm not sure about... I want to hold onto my old assumptions, my old world view, while I try on the new, just in case it doesn't work out. The problem with that is you can't invest fully in something without the "fully" part. You can't, as the gospel story reminds us so vividly, play it safe. When it comes to gardening or congregational development or any other endeavor where we partner with God, the issue is the same. To really commit, you have to give it all you've got.

That's hard for me. Take my garden for example. I had a good time planning it. I was pleased when it was finally time to put in the plants and I could stand them up in their little rows and put on the fertilizer and water. Just doing that felt like a big accomplishment.

But after that interesting time of planting, I had difficulty investing time and energy in the garden. I hadn't figured on organizing my life to check on how the plants were doing every day. I had visions of sitting out in the sun among the blooming flowers and ripening tomatoes in my spare time. I forgot that I rarely have spare time unless I make it!

So the inevitable happened. Even though this garden was right outside my front door, I would often go a week or more without stepping into it. If I thought that a problem was developing (white spots on the tomatoes or strange bugs on the basil), my first reaction was not to charge out and set things right. Instead, I felt inadequate. I really didn't know how to deal with these problems. I found myself making excuses to do other work, to stay inside and ignore the garden completely. I hoped spots and bug problems would resolve themselves.

Thinking back on it now, I see that I needed to spend at least half an hour a day in the garden. Weeding and hoeing, enjoying butterflies and bunnies, and just noticing what's going on should be done continuously and consistently. If I had embraced that discipline (which would not really have been hard to do) I might have noticed the mold on the tomatoes before it ruined one whole vine. I didn't need to know how to cure it right then. I could have taken time to Google the issue and find treatment options. As it was, the problems took over and limited not only my crop, but my enjoyment of the garden.

This coming summer, I'm organizing my time to accommodate my garden and my identity as a gardener. The structure of my life will change to support this new way of being. I really should have been ready to do this reorganization of my life when I first started.

I know so many churches which make the same mistake when doing congregational development. A wonderful job is done by members, mixing in new elements and visioning a future. The little plants of ministry are set into enriched soil and watered well. But no thought is given to how the congregation will continuously and consistently monitor their new way of life. So both old patterns and new problems take over in no time.

Investment in a development process requires ongoing discipline at the level of the congregation's system, i.e. its patterns of relationships. This is not a "rearranging deck chairs on the Titanic" scenario. Commitment takes place in the center of the church and the heart of the congregation. It will change how you do things, and who you are, as a Christian community forever.

WHO'S IN CHARGE?

Responsibility for continuing support of a new system requires that some members take this on as their ministry.

Many congregations have already established governing boards (such as vestries, sessions or councils) responsible for the financial and programmatic life of the church. Could they take on the responsibilities which reorganization demands and make it a priority of their work? If they are willing, and the kind of leaders who delight in supporting and empowering others, this may be the answer.

In some congregations, a separate group (often designated the Ministry Support Team) is assigned tasks specific to the reorganized life of shared ministry. In such cases, the role of team members can be planned for just as any other ministry, with needed gifts and talents specified and time limits established. If the Ministry Support Team model is adopted, care must be taken to lay down lines of communication with the governing board.

For an example of a Ministry Support Team Role description, go to p.

In larger congregations, it makes a lot of sense to have the two oversight groups. In smaller churches, however, it may be that the one team is enough to cover all the various bases needed. (In the tiniest of congregations I have worked with, the matter usually resolves itself. The whole membership is involved in everything, anyway.)

WHAT NEEDS TO BE DONE?

While each congregation must figure out how to reorganize their system in harmony with their own personality and call, there are three areas central to the Mutual Ministry church to take into consideration: 1-Accountability/Celebration, 2-Ongoing Discernment, and 3-Ongoing Support.

In some churches one or more of these elements may already be part of their interactions. In others they may be missing altogether. For the church to flourish however, all congregations must find a way to walk through these areas regularly, no matter how difficult or uncomfortable the discipline.

ACCOUNTABILITY AND CELEBRATION

Accountability and celebration are two sides of the same coin. Holding people accountable means that they have an obligation to report on their work and explain what it is happening. It requires facing problems head-on. Celebrating the ministries of members means that people have a chance to share stories of success and have them praised and built upon.

The prevalent attitude towards accountability in most congregations is to avoid it at all costs. Like the third servant in the parable of the talents, we would rather bury our gifts than risk judgment about how we use them. And, because we have such a hard time acknowledging when there are problems or failures, we also have difficulty celebrating with honesty. Any light shed on the nuts and bolts of our everyday ministry actions seems a bit threatening.

WHY DO WE AVOID ACCOUNTABILITY?

I think it is because, for the majority of people in the pews, church is one of the few safe havens in their lives. This is a place they can come where love is preached as unconditional. It is home for them in a way they have experienced all too rarely in their lives. To be criticized in such a setting feels like being kicked out of paradise.

Because of this attitude, care has to be taken to define accountability as something other than personal criticism. It can never lead to ridicule and shunning. It must be done in the spirit of love. Although this sounds good, congregations have very little experience with actually "speaking the truth in love." We usually opt instead for gossiping behind people's backs in the parking lot.

To change this communal behavior, we need a way to challenge the assumption that accountability and personal rejection go hand in hand. In Community Organizing, there is an acknowledgement of two kinds of community where people are connected through radically different motives. One is the 'private' arena where people are influenced to act out of unconditional love, acceptance, similarity and approval. This is the warm, comfy atmosphere of an ideal home where one is surrounded by like-minded friends and family. Conflict and strife are at a minimum. We all need communities like this in our lives.

The other type of human structure is the 'public' arena where people gather and interact so that they can get things done. In this community, people are motivated by power. They want to connect to others who have the ability, capacity and willingness to act. Here, we need diversity of opinion and experience to see all sides of an issue. Decisions are honed by conflict and debate. In this public sphere, respect is the most valuable coinage in personal relationships. It is earned as people are held accountable for their actions and learn to refine their own power.

While most of the time people place church in the private sphere, I believe it is the one community in our world which is actually called to have a foot in both the private and the public arenas of life. If we give up the personal relationships of unconditional love and acceptance, we violate the Gospel. If we ignore or avoid the public motivations and connections of the church, we give up our power to influence the world, and our greatest opportunity to be partners with God.

ACCOUNTABILITY IN LOVE

The key to balancing our stance in the church as participating in both the public and private arenas lies in being able to create an atmosphere of accountability which never sacrifices love. But realistically, how can we do this? It may be that the mental model of "edit-ability" proposed by Joseph Meyers in his book *Organic Community* will help our members get their heads and hearts around this concept.[48]

Meyers says, "Accountants keep records. Editors wipe away errors while keeping the voice of the author."[49] If, in our congregations, we could replace the assumption of accountability as criticism and rejection with a mental model of edit-ability, our foundational stance would change. We would assume the body of people around us values and does not want to lose our contribution. This stance of "positive interdependence"[50] would help create a safe environment for all of our ministry efforts.

Edit-ability also reinforces the mental model of the radical equality of ministers. It insists that whatever person or groups we report to are not our superiors but our co-workers. Because we are all partnering with God, they have a vested interest in making each one of us successful. This is the team model lived out in the effort of everyday ministry.

Redefining accountability as the work of editing also shifts our focus as we observe ministry in action. When an editor works with an author, faith in the person's writing has already been declared. The book now becomes the project to which both author and editor apply their energy, collaborating to make it as good as possible. In the same way, ministers are the authors of the ministry to which they have been called...but they are not called to do it alone. Instead of judging the worthiness of a person, the ministry editor pays attention to the project and what is being done.

A good editor will also realize that the "re-write" is still the work of the author. Pointing out problem areas does not mean solving them, although suggestions and brainstorming are often helpful to get a minister back on track. In extreme cases, where it is evident that a "bad" call has been issued and the minister is not in a place where he or she can succeed, the editing process helps assign a project that is more appropriate

Ultimately, the communal assumption of edit-ability rests on the understanding that we are made in the image of God and are therefore fundamentally good. This unconditional acceptance of people is the orientation of the private sphere. But in edit-ability this assumption of human worth meshes with the public arena as we create an environment where all people are empowered to partner well with God and the congregation.

Does this sound possible for the congregation to do? It may take some intense conversation to move in this direction. It may also take some practice, with forgiveness being asked when people's feelings are hurt or misunderstandings occur. The payoff will be that close observation of ministries will happen and both prevention of disaster and rejoicing in success will take place more often.

As ministers are held more accountable, two other elements of reorganization are also going to be imperative: ongoing discernment and ongoing education equip a team to meet problem areas head on.

ONGOING DISCERNMENT

Ongoing discernment has two focal points: The first lies in the members already gathered. There will be times (and these should be regular and scheduled) when people are invited to reconsider what they are doing in partnership with God. Are the some members at the end of their commitment time and wanting to try another venue? Is there a minister who is just not thriving? Either the Ministry Support Team or the governing board needs to ask these questions on a regular basis. An annual Mutual Ministry Review (MMR) may provide the time and space for the whole congregation to regularly consider such ongoing discernment.

See p. 220 for a sample agenda for MMRs – Mutual Ministry Reviews

The other focal point of ongoing discernment centers on the people who are just joining the congregation. The sooner new members can find a ministry in the church that is uniquely suited for their gifts and talents, the sooner they will really take root in the church.

The tool of Relational Meetings, which comes out of the Community Organizing discipline, is ideal for getting to know new comers at a level which will allow initial discernment. Because these one-on-one conversations get to the heart of what motivates a person, the listener will quickly be able to identify areas of true interest. If your congregation has not used relational meetings before, this might be a good time to train some people in the method to use intentionally with anyone interested in becoming a member.[51]

The common wisdom of church development is that anyone entering a church will need to find at least a handful of people to call friends within a few months, if they are to stay around. Your listeners should be ready to introduce the newcomer to other members with interests in similar areas as soon as possible. In this way, people become rooted in relationships which can grow into shared ministries.

When a new ministry is identified for either a new member or an established member, it is important to acknowledge this publicly. The whole congregation benefits from seeing discernment in action among them. They will continue to encourage each other into deeper relationship with God. It will become the normative stance of the whole congregation to be on the outlook for callings.

ONGOING EDUCATION

All of the points made in the previous chapter under "Training and Education" need to be reviewed after people have settled into the ministries to which they have been called: 1-The congregation is responsible for getting members what they need to succeed, 2-All ministries require foundational knowledge of and the ability to articulate the Christian faith, and 3-Learning in groups is more beneficial than individual education. Instead of just trusting that plans made in these areas have been followed through, a regular review of how these efforts are going is imperative.

My experience is that, while intentions for education and training are usually good, investing time in these areas when the demands of life are upon us is difficult. The community organizing motto "power precedes programs" is worth remembering and reflecting on, if this is a propensity of your congregation.

Think of education and training as the water and sunshine of your church garden. If you skimp on either, your people won't have the energy to do the ministries they are called to. Burn out and discouragement is high in congregations which are not vigilant about making sure their ministers are well nourished in Christian education and have ongoing training in their ministry areas.

Much of our power for ministry is supplied through formation with other members of the congregation. Therefore, the most important element of ongoing education to establish and keep up is that of a continuing program (like LifeCycles[52] or EfM/Education for Ministry[53]) which invites people to develop their relationship with God and others as they learn together. Programs like these emphasize the equality of all before God and therefore support the fundamental aspects of ministering together as a community.

How to Reorganize?

Whether you simply add the three tasks above to already existing groups like your vestry, session or council, or form a Ministry Support Team whose focus will be exclusively on accountability/celebration, discernment and education, the question remains: How will you do it? We've been doing Church basically the same way for a long, long time. Now we are called not only to redevelop our congregations but to do it at systemic level. How can we pull this off?

Let's go back to the parable of the talents, which perhaps we should rename "the parable of changing systemically". The three servants in the story were being given a new call in their lives. No longer were they just following orders. Now they had the opportunity to step out of the role of slave and into the role of investor. No one handed them a certificate saying that they were ready to do this. They didn't have access to a lot of education about the stock market or an MBA. They didn't even know when the master was returning and so had no real parameters in terms of how long they might try on this new identity.

The two servants who were successful simply began acting like investors. They took the money they had been given and did something with it. We don't get to see behind the storyline and so don't know how long it took them to figure out how to do this or how many times they failed to make more money before they got it right. All we are allowed to know is that when the master finally did come back, they had been successful at not only making him some more money, but at becoming investors. He was confident enough in their new identities that he invited them to become his partners.

The third servant never acted. He hid the money and he hid his potential. Invited to be an investor, he chose to stay a servant. And so, his fate was to become even less than a slave.

SELF-ORGANIZATION

The thing about systemic change, change at the level of identity in people or organizations, is that it requires risk. No one can tell you exactly how to do it, because it is a creative act which must arise from the community itself. But given a chance, it will rise. Donella Meadows, in discussing the characteristics of healthy systems in her book *Thinking in Systems*, calls this the principle of self-organization.[54]

Meadows says that the most successful self-organization focuses on a simple principle or rule, building on it over and over again. In scientific circles, this is shown graphically in patterns called fractals. Think of a snowflake or a fern. In each of these, there is a simple pattern repeated over and over in different areas and at different levels.

In communities, when organization is elegant and functional at the same time, it's because a fundamental principle has been discovered and reproduced in every area of life. This principle is deeper than the vision of the group. It is more like a relational mental model that everyone adopts. For example, an army functions because it adheres to the principle of obedience and loyalty in all ranks. This is reproduced from the lowest relationships between private and sergeants up to the relationship between 4-star generals and presidents. It is such an accepted factor that it is usually not even noticed until it is violated.(A prime example of this violation recently occurred when a general spoke disparagingly of the President in the presence of reporters, and then had to resign his commission.)

What is the fundamental, absolutely foundational, principle in Mutual Ministry? If we go back to the Baptismal Covenant, I think we will see it in this simple rule: We are all called to be God's beloved partners.

This principle of loving partnership is true on the individual level, between each of us and other people. It is true between us and creation. And it is true between us and God.

It is also true on the congregational level: between the choir and the Sunday school, the mission board and the altar guild, etc. (If this book were concerned with the national church structures, we could make a case for it being necessary on those levels as well!) The equality of partnership in God's love is foundational to every connection and relationship as we seek to live completely into this identity.

A group which has taken on the tasks of oversight, supporting all the members of the congregation in their ministries, will want this value of beloved partnership to be the basis of every decision that they make. In planning for the future and following God's unique call for each congregation, it will be the guiding light focusing each goal and objective.

In my experience, after identifying and committing to the basic relational mental model, two more things are necessary in order for the congregation members to throw themselves fully into the identity of a Mutual Ministry congregation and succeed. The first is the rethinking of hierarchy and the second is commitment to practice. Let's look first at hierarchy.

HIERARCHY

My own context is the Episcopal Church which is unabashed in its love affair with a particular kind of hierarchy. We may talk about the equality of all the baptized, and even believe it, but we dress up our priests and bishops in cloth of gold with elaborate hats and capes…even while making them walk at the end of processions. Our collective assumption is of a vertical hierarchy with Bishops at the top and laity at the bottom.

This is not the only way to be stuck in a vertical, top-down vision of hierarchy. In denominations which have surrendered the pomp and circumstance of the ordained orders for the more staid and sober offices of pastor, the glorification of education and the elevated status of preachers often exists. Even in community churches, the pulpit is often laden with an expectation of honor and respect which is over and above dignity given to other members.

Does the radical equality of Mutual Ministry demand we do away with hierarchy completely? If we do, we give up a strategy for life which has worked since the first fish crawled out of the sea. Hierarchy is most simply defined as systemic organization into smaller groups which pursue goals supporting a centralized and communal goal. It has made possible the growth and vitality of complex organizations. Our challenge is to give up "vertical" hierarchy and embrace a different configuration of these specialized groups.

Horizontal or circular hierarchy is the radical equality which we talked about in the former chapter, now extended to groups as well as individuals. To treat each ministry group in the church as equal and invaluable to the function of the whole will stretch us a bit further as God's partners. Our mental model must accept that the maintenance crew is just as important as the choir or the ordained pastors. We are all working together for the good of the God's reign and therefore deserve the same level of support. It is Paul's metaphor of the body expanded into organization of the community.

Whatever group in the congregation is charged with oversight of the systemic reorganization, they will be the team which must ultimately model the practice of horizontal hierarchy and the radical equality of all. The care that they take with all ministers and ministries must be of the same depth and quality. When considering what resources are available, they must not play favorites with those conventionally designated as the "higher" ministries but give, as St. Paul would say, more dignity to those parts which by nature are more vulnerable and considered lowly.

This way of being is most difficult to realize in a congregation where a paid rector/pastor is serving. That person is a visible symbol of the assumption of vertical hierarchy. In such cases, embracing a model of horizontal or circular hierarchy can only be done if the rector/pastor has made the switch first. Indeed, if ordained ministers embrace completely the identity of equal and beloved partnership with all others, it will inspire the rest of the members to make the change with greater confidence.

PRACTICING MUTUAL MINISTRY

When the congregation is committed to living fully into the relationship of loving partnership with God, on both the individual and hierarchical levels, what practical steps will be helpful? This is a question of central importance, because this is where the discipline of the living into the identity is established. I can think all day about the importance of going out into my garden to keep an eye on how things are progressing (or not). I can talk about it with other gardeners and even preach it to new gardeners. Nothing will change in my garden, however, until I follow through with action. Actual practice will inform my learning and train me in a different way of being. It is the only thing which will ultimately make a difference to my plants.

While every congregation must figure out its own discipline, here are two guidelines which congregations committed to Mutual Ministry have found helpful:

1) First of all, the group which takes on the responsibility for accountability/celebration, ongoing discernment and ongoing education needs to meet on a regular basis. This team considers the elements central to restructuring in each ministry. Gathering at least every month for oversight is most helpful. It may be advisable to meet more often (weekly or bi-weekly) in the beginning to fully consolidate the team. The ability of this group to model consistent interest in and support for all ministries enhances the shift in assumptions which the whole community is making toward radical

equality. Transparency and consistency in communication with the rest of the members will reinforce the focus of Mutual Ministry.

2) Secondly, it will be most helpful if members of the oversight group are involved in ongoing Christian formation. They may want to engage in a weekly or bi-weekly study together (as in the LifeCycles model). Or they may want to study as part of a larger group, and come together once a month for business. Either way, attentiveness to the ongoing growth of their life in Christ will model and support the congregation's priority of Christian formation for all.

Other than these two suggestions, the field is wide open for how this group supporting new life in the church will function. Jump in and begin practicing! After you act, reflect on what has happened and refine your practice to modify and enhance results.

WHEN DO WE ADD THIS?

The question of when to add this element of systemic reorganization to the mix as you engage in congregational development will need to be answered by each congregation as they consider the context of their work. For some, it will be important to include the concept of a loving partnership with God as the relational template which informs the effort from the beginning. For others, positive experiences of thinking about and acting as a congregation in new ways will need to come first. They then can build on their experience, deliberately and slowly, creating acceptance of such a radically different identity. For most congregations, a little challenging theology can be proposed up front and then the themes of radical equality and loving partnership can be revisited throughout the development process.

In my experience, systemic reorganization has sometimes been an element imposed on congregations which are perceived as failing. They were told to become Mutual Ministry congregations without much other guidance. Some of them worked hard to embrace the mental model of radical equality on all levels and, with lots of practice, trial and error (and a lot of forgiveness to themselves when they didn't follow through) they were able to move in this direction successfully. These churches have thrived in ministry.

Other congregations, when forced into reorganizing because they could no longer afford a seminary-trained priest or pastor, conformed as well as they could to what they thought they were being asked to do. However, they never confronted the assumptions and mental models underlying their understanding of the systems of Church. Although they did what they thought would bring about change, their practices had very shallow roots, not nurtured by the values of the members. Most of these congregations have never stopped wanting to go back to the old system. At best, they succeeded at survival.

The point here is that if you want to add this element to your mix early in the development process, be aware that not everyone will understand what you are trying to get at. It cannot be imposed. The most one can do is lay it on the surface of the community and invite members to engage with it.

Systemic reorganization is the hardest and deepest change that the congregation must embrace. While not as dramatic as communal formation or the discernment process, it is about transformation at the communal heart of the congregation. As such, it must be sustained and practiced on an ongoing basis. It becomes the way of life for the community gathered in Christ's name, nourishing all decisions and actions.

Without systemic reorganization, everything else you have done to promote development will be lost, eventually. It will be like a garden with no one to care for it. Some roots may still send forth shoots for a few years, but with no one to tend them, wild growth, early decay and general chaos will overtake the plants. In a few years your plot will simply be another patch of overgrown yard.

An identity of being beloved partners with God is possible only with disciplined practice of the values which support Mutual Ministry. The Christian community as a whole is defined by how it chooses to live out its relationship with God. We make this choice for God, empowered by the knowledge that God has chosen us through Christ, to be his hands and heart in this world.

CHAPTER 8 — CONVERSATION STARTERS

As you think about systemic reorganization, plan first to address the assumptions of the congregation's relational structure. Only after you are clear that the church community is ready to live out of the values of equal ministry and beloved partnership can a real shift in how you "do" church happen. Practical ways of being will arise out of practicing different ways of being together.

1) Does your congregation see itself predominately as a private or a public community? What are the pros and cons of the stance it has taken? If you were to invite a broader view of church living in both the public and private worlds, how would that look?

2) Do you agree that the foundational orientation of the church should be that of a beloved partnership with God and each other? Is this how you are relating with each other at the moment? If not, what would indicate a change in this direction?

3) Which of the three areas central to restructuring (accountability/celebration, ongoing discernment, and ongoing education) will be a challenge to you? Why? What kind of oversight team might be most helpful in bringing these into your communal life?

4) How do you define hierarchy? How might you want to refine your understanding?

5) What do you think might really change in your life together as you take root in this new way of living together? Consider liturgy, fellowship, outreach and any other areas of life you have as a community.

6) In your context, how and when might it be best to introduce this invitation to be fully God's beloved partners?

CHAPTER 9

TAKING ROOT

> *"I planted the seed, Apollos watered the plants, but God made you grow. It's not the one who plants or the one who waters who is at the center of this process but God, who makes things grow."* (1 Corinthians 3: 6-7)

My husband and I owned five houses before we built the house in which we now live. At all these places we made extensive landscape renovations…mostly due to my husband's love of getting outdoors and playing in the dirt! Our first home (a little rectangle in a trailer park) was beautified by irises and we successfully grew cucumbers and zucchini there. At other addresses, we pulled down dead trees and planted new ones. We have relocated bushes and begun flower beds. We have taken out grass for xeriscaping and added grass to soften a harsh landscape. At every location we found ourselves building on what had gone before, modifying and beautifying, and then letting it go for the next owner to improve a bit more.

Landscaping around the house we built has been a rather different experience for us. We took a desolate and undeveloped little plot of land and gave free rein to our imaginations. It has been an evolving project for the three years we have been here…and will continue to progress as long as we stay.

When we finally move on, I think this will be the most difficult place to leave. It is so much more "ours" than any of the other places we have lived. But really, I know that is a fantasy. Landscapes and gardens, just like churches, have a life of their own. They may be shaped by gardeners who come and go, but ultimately they belong to God. Their continuity is beyond any individual effort. We, no matter how we love our gardens or our congregations, are only part of the environment at a given time. We are destined to go our way and let the community of plants, or the community of saints, continue on without us.

Does this mean we are unimportant? No. Paul and Apollos were not unimportant, and neither are we. Very often we don't even know how or where the influence of our care has taken root. The central challenge then, in congregations as in gardens, is to be sure that the soil, the underlying system of relationships which will sustain growth and vitality, is sound and nurturing. If we can commit ourselves to this work which is often not flashy or even noticed (residing as it does in the dark and hidden humus of our life together), we will have accomplished something lasting indeed.

REVIEW OF UNIVERSAL ORIENTATIONS FOR DEVELOPMENT

This book started with the premise that there are some fundamental orientations which are necessary to engage in congregational development. Before considering the ingredients needed to revitalize the soil of congregations, I suggested raising the planting bed by making sure four planks were in place to create capacity, i.e. the room to hold dramatically new elements of church life. The framework necessary to support a change as fundamentally systemic as Mutual Ministry includes these four universal orientations or commitments:

1) The ability to converse
2) A willingness to know and to be known
3) Practicing a connection to God
4) Proactive patience

If you are experiencing a stall out with your development process, one of these planks may not have been sufficiently developed or may, for some reason, have been knocked out of place.

How do you estimate orientation and commitment in a congregation? You might want to go back to Chapter Two and review the descriptions of these "planks". Then, retake the little quiz provided in the "Conversation Starter" section. Your study group or development team will notice whether the congregation seems to be avoiding, or never really spent time developing, one of these qualities.

If one of these areas is underdeveloped, shift the attention of your development process to address it as soon as possible. Don't go forward with adding more ingredients of development to the congregational soil until there is a commitment to do so with these four orientations intact. If you do try to forge ahead without tackling these fundamentals, your work will, sooner or later, fall apart. It will be the effort of just a few people instead of the whole community's work.

Most congregations need to revisit these four orientations and recommit at regular intervals to being a community called by God. It is the maintenance work of the church. But each time the congregation pledges itself anew to conversing, knowing, connecting, and practicing patience, these attitudes become more deeply rooted and the community's dedication to its own development is strengthened.

REVIEW OF DEVELOPMENT ELEMENTS

With the commitment and orientation of the congregation intact, let's take a moment to review the ingredients of the congregation's soil...the enriching elements that we have come to understand are fundamental to the health and growth of the Christian community.

We considered **"Playing with the Need to Change"**, which is an exploration of congregational motivation. Knowing what is driving our interest in doing things differently greatly enhances both our commitment to doing the work which is needed and our persistence in continuing until the system is supporting change. While this is an ingredient which may be added at any time, the conversational exercises which bring us understanding of motivation are helpful to fold in at the beginning of the development process. Once dialogue is exchanged for debate, a congregation may revisit this element with ease, both formally and informally.

"Exploring the Congregation's Past and Present Identity" is an additive which invites the group to claim both the positive and negative aspects of their collective personality. Acknowledging that each church community is unique and called by a God who seems to love the quirky and unconventional, we seek to find the foundation of who we are as a community so that we can build on what is positive in it. This again is an exercise based on the ability to share different viewpoints and insights without competing. The recommended workshops deepen the art of conversation and give the group common language with which to describe themselves. Once a year is about the limit of what a congregation can stand with this element. Even once a year may be too often to do a full-fledged exploration...but a simple time line and storytelling event can be invaluable for inviting new members into the heart of the parish family, as well as reminding long time members of the church's identity.

The element of **"Communal Formation"** may be the most unfamiliar ingredient for church developers, dealing as it does with the call of the whole congregation and not just the individuals in it. This element asks the question "What is God calling us as a congregation to be and do?" The patience of the group may be tested by the length of time which is recommended for this process...but if linked to the fundamental stance of "proactive patience" and understood as being necessary for systemic change, communal formation may come to be embraced as a way of life.

"A **Plan to Learn**" is the element which takes visioning a step further, making it a vehicle for the ongoing developmental journey. For churches which have had long range planning workshops, the concept of planning as a map for life-long learning (instead of concrete goals to control the future), may seem mystifying. A sense of God's call to the congregation as articulated in communal formation will offer clarity.

The element of **"Gifts and Needs Discernment"** includes four separate aspects: 1) discerning the gifts of the members, 2) discerning ministries, 3) calling, and 4) training and education. The application of this ingredient contains the most crucial step by step formula in this book, since my experience is that discernment can be harmful if not applied carefully and completely. Whenever your congregation is ready to engage this element, take time to think through the process and commit to finishing the course.

"Systemic Reorganization" is the addition to our soil which acknowledges that the way we connect through our relationships in a community is at the heart of all deep change. Building in the discipline to do the work needed to sustain relational development is both basic and challenging. It calls for deeper commitment to new communal assumptions, mental models and patterns in groups. This is the ingredient which will root the fundamental relational principal of Mutual Ministry (that we are invited to be God's beloved partners) in your congregation.

ALL SHALL BE WELL

Reviewing the universal orientations and the development elements is my attempt to give you some perspective on the process of congregational development in a Mutual Ministry style. It is not possible to address all of these elements in a short period of time. It is also not possible to know exactly where the journey of development will lead a congregation. So in the work of congregational development, pacing and letting go of unrealistic expectations is important (especially for the health and sanity of the developer/gardener).

> **PACING**

It's understandable, in our quick-fix world, to desire a more clearly outlined and faster paced program. But consider this: This process of congregational development is similar to a 12 step programs like AA and Al Anon. Rehabilitation may set an individual or family on the road to health. However, if there are not fundamental and sustained changes in the way people choose to live together, there will not be true and deep healing or continued maturation. Congregational development and 12-step programs are both lifelong developmental processes which provide guidance and support at all stages of recovery...even when participants have achieved more health than is normally seen in our society.

Developing a congregation in a Mutual Ministry style is this kind of lifelong commitment to continued healing and spiritual growth. There is actually plenty of time to do all that is encompassed in this book, and come back and do it again and again. This is because congregations are not ever expected to finish. The garden must be prepared, planted, weeded and nurtured and harvested every year, with the fallow season of winter respected and allowed for as well. The church must also observe its seasons of preparation, growth, harvest and rest knowing that to live is to continue the cycle at ever deepening levels.

LETTING GO

There is also plenty of time for this kind of development in the Church because when you (the ministry developer or development group) are gone it will be someone else's turn to lead this process, taking up the spade and hoe. Mutual Ministry is at heart a partnership with God and, through God, with each other. It is imperative that as many people as possible in the congregation take responsibility for the development of their Christian community. As I have heard several proponents of Mutual Ministry say, "Make sure that the end product has as many fingerprints on it as possible!"

Much of this book is about how to be sure the church is raising up and folding in leaders all the time. In building a network of committed lay and ordained ministers in your congregation, when the inevitable happens and central leaders leave, farewells can be said without panic or regret. As a developer or team of developers, you can exit (either to heaven or the next community which calls) knowing that the soil is rich and nurturing and that growth will go on in your absence.

That's a good feeling: knowing that you have left this corner of God's kingdom more fruitful than you when you arrived. You may not have gotten what you originally intended. Your garden may have wonderful tomatoes and yet never have produced a pepper worth eating. Your congregation may have a vibrant life and positive impact on all in the surrounding community, yet still struggle to pay the bills. Yet, I assure you, your partnership with God has been productive.

And God will stay around to see that there are ministers to attend to the next round of tilling and weeding and watering. Where you have followed in the footsteps of Paul and Apollos, know others will walk too. Trust the Holy Spirit knows what is needed and will call that forth from the community. In our partnership with God, after all, is a occupy the junior position. As Julian of Norwich heard God say: "All shall be well and all shall be well and all manner of thing shall be well."

CHAPTER 9 — CONVERSATION STARTERS

In some ways this chapter should have been in the beginning of the book. A succinct review of what is needed for congregational development in a Mutual Ministry style might have been helpful (or terrifying!) as you began thinking about this process. I hoped, however, to woo the reader into seeing the various components and orientations as fascinating, in and of themselves.

Like all organic processes however, there are very few elements which are distinct and unaffected by what proceeds and follows them. As you have reached this summary chapter, now is the time to decide what to do with the material you have learned (if, indeed, you have not already begun the work). The conversation starters below will give you some direction as you consider what steps to take next.

1) As you look at your own and your team's future, will you be around long enough to dig into this work? If you plan on being present only for a year or two, what components would make the most difference to the health of relationships in the congregation, so that the process can be sustained after you leave? If you will be present for the long haul (10+ years), what sequence makes the most sense for a sustained effort?

2) Think about your relationship and commitment to the congregation. What measure of success is most important to you and others in your development group? How does this fit with your role of being God's "junior" partner?

3) As you think about beginning or continuing a congregational development process, go back over the discussions you have had at the end of the previous chapters. Is there consensus around where you need to start? If not, how will you reach a decision?

4) Consider also the timing of a development process. What season is your congregation in now? Has it been lying fallow and now needs to wake up and begin preparations for growth? Are certain areas of the congregation growing and producing, which need to be nurtured and protected? Have some initiatives just begun, so that care needs to be taken not to dislodge them?

NEW GROWTH IN GOD'S GARDEN

SECTION II:

THE TOOL SHED

RESOURCES FOR

CONGREGATIONAL DEVELOPMENT

IN A MUTUAL MINISTRY STYLE

Material in this book is also available
as a downloadable electronic file
with a license to reproduce.

For more information
go to www.LeaderResources.org
or call 1-800-941-2218

INTRODUCTION

> " ... God is able to bless you abundantly, so that in all things at all times, having all that you need, you will abound in every good work." (2 Corinthians 9:6-8)

One Saturday morning, I got up full of energy and decided to attack the weeds growing in our backyard patio area, which is made of flagstone. We had been trying to get the cracks between the stones filled in with different varieties of thyme. The thyme was doing well, but I had been negligent and now weeds of all kinds had crept in as well. I grabbed my new trowel with the bright green padded handle and headed out to do battle.

Half an hour (and many little holes) later, my husband stuck his head out the door and asked, "Why are you digging up weeds with that? Why don't you use the weeding tool?" Since it was clear from my look of befuddlement that I had no idea what he was talking about, he obligingly fetched it for me.

The weeding tool, it turns out, is an unassuming piece of metal a bit bigger than a screw driver with a forked head. Applied correctly, it ingeniously rips weeds out of the ground with roots intact, and without digging craters. I cast down my trowel, picked up this little tool, and had the patio weeded in no time.

"HAVING ALL THAT YOU NEED…"

Paul gives a promise to the early congregations that God will give them everything necessary to succeed. Most of us, however, call this promise into question when facing the task of Congregational Development. I hear it from all sides: "We would be able to do something about this parish if we just had more money, more people, more support." The truth for us, just as it was for that little Corinthian congregation, is that God is able to give us everything we need to grow abundantly in every good work.

God is able to give. But are we able to receive? My guess is that we are a little conflicted in this area of "receiving". There are may be several reasons for this. One may be the issue of size and energy…i.e. we really don't have much to work with. The second may be related to the appropriateness of the tools we are trying to use in our particular context. Before we go on to the tools themselves, let's take a look at these two issues.

EXPANDING THE BOUNDARIES

There does seem to be a point when a congregation may really have too few members to think about doing much more than keep the doors open on Sunday. What does St. Paul's promise mean to them? Can they expect to have everything that they need to be successful, i.e. not only keep the doors open but have a lively, vital and energetic ministry which impacts the world about them?

I think that the church in such a situation can expect to have all they need, but they may have to expand the notion of their own boundaries to receive the gift. While Paul was speaking to one small congregation struggling in Corinth when he said God would bless them with all they needed, we know that the small churches scattered across the country were concerned about each other. Purses were collected when one group was in need. Paul himself was a gift and blessing shuttling back and forth between them, knitting them together into a larger community. And so it is with our individual churches. None of us stands alone. Even larger congregations benefit from joining forces with others.

Many mainline judicatories these days are looking to combine congregations in small towns, sometimes across denominational lines. Churches may be "yoked" by providing an ordained minister of one of the denominations to serve both communities. Other times, expenses are curtailed and gifts shared by condensing the congregations into one building and fellowship which has the blessing of both (and in some cases more than two) different brands of Christianity.

More productive than these directed mergers, however, is when congregations in an area join together out of their own sense of being called to be stronger partners with God. These groups, whether of one denomination or of several, have found out how to build power…and so their ministry becomes greater than the sum of individual congregations.

Also interesting are those congregations in small towns which are playing down (but not giving up) their denominational status to find their main identity in serving all people in the extended community, whether members of the church or not. These parishes see the boundaries of their church expanding out and incorporating everybody in a radius of a several miles. As they develop their Christian community, they have a much larger population than the figures on the Sunday service book would suggest. Maintaining that open view while at the same time holding on to their roots, they will have access to both denominational gifts and the talents and skills of people not usually connected with the congregation.

If your congregation is feeling impoverished, consider how you might become open to gifts stashed in strange places or under unfamiliar guises. Listen to voices which may be offering wisdom and partnership from afar.

CHOOSING THE RIGHT TOOL

Another issue hindering our ability to receive all that is needed is our obtuseness about reaching for the most suitable tool. Sometimes, like in my weeding incident, we grab (or lust after) the shiniest new tool without thought as to whether it's actually the best tool for the job. In the congregation, this may be the latest education series that the church down the block is using successfully or the newest program being pushed by the denominational heads. When we fall victim to the "shiniest tool" syndrome, we react to the tool rather than to the job we are intending to do.

Even if it's a proper implement for the kind of job we are tackling, we also must ask, "Is it appropriate to our context?" Riding lawn mowers are wonderful tools if you have acres of lawn, but impractical for most city lots (even if they do look like fun!). With congregational development, expensive tools used by larger congregations often just overwhelm people in smaller, more intimate settings. Conversely, a process which has been developed for smaller groups may be unhelpful in large congregations. There are no "one size fits all" church development tools.

The biggest issue when developing a Mutual Ministry church, however, is acknowledging that the majority of tools for church development have been crafted for use in institutions with vertical hierarchies. Those of us interested in a more circular and equal distribution of power may find ourselves at cross-purposes when engaging these programs.

This is the most critical aspect to pay attention to when choosing a development tool. It is so easy to fall back into the mental models of reliance on the ordained clergy and rigid, constricted roles. In a Mutual Ministry setting (or a congregation which desires such an environment), we want to pick or create the kind of tools which will first and foremost help us build relationships of equal partnership.

Think of this as being the kind of gardener who is committed to ecologically sound practices. Even though a product is touted as having miraculous ability to help your plants resist bugs, if it is hurtful to the environment you would be loath to use it. There is always another way to accomplish bug control.

In the Mutual Ministry church, there is always a way to progress which encourages us to fulfill the call to be God's equal and beloved partners. The means must be consistent and integral with the desired end.

While most of us are hesitant to mess with programs that others have created and used to good effect, I would urge you to not feel like any of the tools offered here is sacrosanct. Embrace your creativity and modify these offerings. If nothing here appeals to you, recall the basics of good conversation and learning as an act of mutual exploration and discovery. Then create your own programs. And share what you have done with the wider community of congregations which are on this journey.

Have fun!

THE WORLD CAFÉ — OVERVIEW

Description: The World Café is a method of structuring conversations to ensure participation by all with a deep level of acceptance of differing viewpoints, and encouragement for real creativity and collaborative thinking.

Format: You will need twelve people minimum for this exercise and a time period of at least 90 minutes. There seems to be no maximum number, but the logistics get more complicated as numbers increase.

Materials Needed: Tables which will accommodate four (this is the number of people talking together in the small groups) and which have large sheets of paper and drawing materials on them are the main requirement. You will also need a place to gather the whole group to begin and end the process.

A table host is needed for each small group, and while this person must be prepared, the training is not complicated or rigorous.

Careful preparation for the event is very important, especially the crafting of deep questions.

Indications for Use: The World Café is very helpful when a congregation is learning the difference between debate and conversation. Begin with interesting but less heated issues and then move to more stressful subjects.

This is also a great method for initiating conversation with a larger unit around issues which are being explored by a small study group (like a congregational formation group). Questions posed should refer to what the smaller set is working on. In the program "Rooted in God" such questions are suggested at the end of each session.

Eventually, a congregation might use the World Café whenever it becomes apparent that there are differing points of view about a particular question. It may become the preferred method of getting everyone's thoughts out and creating novel solutions.

Cautions: Fewer than twelve people make this method difficult to appreciate, as you lose the experience of mixing people up to ask the question a second and third time.

Trying to shorten the exercise to less than 90 minutes also limits the effectiveness of this method. While many people want to slip in a World Café as a kind of secondary piece to a decision making process, its strength lies in making the goal of conversing deeply primary… and this takes time.

Directions and More Information: The web site http://www.theworldcafe.com is very thorough. See the Resource Guide, reprinted here, for a quick overall introduction.

A RESOURCE GUIDE FOR THE WORLD CAFÉ

by Juanita Brown and the World Café Community[55]

HOSTING CONVERSATIONS THAT MATTER AT THE WORLD CAFÉ

To help you find your way through this World Café Resource Guide, here's what you'll encounter:

- The Power of Conversation to Create the Future
- What Is The World Café?
- Six Key Principles for Hosting a World Café Conversation
- The Role of the Overall Café Host and the Table Host
- Is the World Café More Than Just Talk?
- Materials to Support Café Hosting
- Where to Go for Additional Information
- Assumptions Underlying The World Café
- Café Etiquette
- Café Set Up and Supplies

THE POWER OF CONVERSATION TO CREATE THE FUTURE

Since our earliest ancestors gathered in circles around the warmth of a fire, conversation has been a core process for discovering what we care about. It's how we've always shared our knowledge, imagined our futures and created communities of commitment. The meanings we make in conversation and the coordinated action that emerges naturally from them help to shape our lives.

Many large change efforts began when people sat down together for informal conversations in living rooms, kitchens, cafés, and church halls. Consider the sewing circles and Committees of Correspondence that helped birth the American Republic, as well as the cafés and salons that spawned the French Revolution. Consider the Scandinavian study circles that stimulated an economic and social renaissance in Northern Europe. Consider the church gatherings where the civil rights movement was born.

In light of recent world events, networks of conversation and committed action are springing up around the globe as we face the critical social, economic, political and environmental challenges of our time. This is how change happens. People in small groups, both face to face and in online communities spread seed ideas for new conversations, creative possibilities and collective action in ever widening networks. What if there was an easy-to-use approach for developing dynamic networks of focused conversation in order to create living knowledge and new possibilities for action even in very large groups? World Café conversations are designed to do just that.

WHAT IS THE WORLD CAFÉ?

The World Café is an intentional way to create a living network of conversations around questions that matter. It is a creative **methodology** for hosting authentic conversations in groups of all sizes. You join several other people at a café-style table or in a small conversation cluster exploring a question or issue that really matters to your life, work or community. Others are sitting at nearby café tables or in small conversation clusters exploring similar questions at the same time. You won't be sitting for too long, however, because half the excitement of being part of a World Café conversation is the opportunity to move to another group or café table, visit with new people and cross-pollinate ideas and insights.

As the conversations connect together, collective knowledge grows and evolves. A sense of the larger whole becomes real. The wisdom of the group becomes more visible.

The World Café is also a useful **metaphor** for noticing how we learn, share knowledge, make meaning and co-evolve our futures through the living networks of conversation in which we participate. Just as fish don't see the water in which they swim, we often don't see the webs of conversation we engage in and their importance to the future of our organizations and communities as living systems. In a World Café gathering, people have the opportunity to experience these critical, but usually invisible learning networks more intentionally. When you come right down to it, living networks of conversation lie at the heart of our capacity as a human community to create the futures we want rather than being forced to live with the futures we get.

Thousands of people have experienced both the methodology and the metaphor of the World Café in settings ranging from crowded hotel ballrooms with 1200 people to cozy intimate living rooms with just a dozen folks present. Leadership Cafés, Knowledge Cafés, Strategy Cafés, and Discovery Cafés have been hosted in large multi-national corporations as well as in small non-profit organizations using the World Café format and operating principles. World Café sessions have been conducted in as little as 90 minutes. Other sessions have lasted several days.

The purposes of each of these cafés, whatever they are named, have been as diverse as the people attending them. Yet the World Café process itself has demonstrated a remarkable capacity to foster authentic conversation among people who may have never met and who have had no formal dialogue training.

The World Café is designed on the assumption that people already have within them the wisdom and creativity to confront even the most difficult challenges. Given the appropriate context and focus, it is possible for members to access this deeper knowledge about what's important. Our research has shown that there are six operating principles underlying World Café-style conversations. When these six principles are used *in combination,* they have the capacity to foster collaborative dialogue, strengthen community, spark creative insight and create new possibilities for constructive action.

SIX KEY PRINCIPLES FOR HOSTING AN EFFECTIVE WORLD CAFÉ CONVERSATION

Hosting a World Café conversation is not hard. Creating an exciting café conversation is limited only by your imagination. Café conversations have happened in living rooms, school rooms, ballrooms, church parlors, universities, neighborhood cafés, corporate retreats, senior citizen centers and even in tents! The café format is flexible and adapts to many different circumstances, based on a few simple operating principles. When the following six principles are used *together,* the magic of the World Café experience is more likely to occur.

WORLD CAFÉ OPERATING PRINCIPLES

1. Create Hospitable Space
2. Explore Questions that Matter
3. Encourage Everyone to Contribute
4. Connect Diverse People and Ideas
5. Listen Together for Insights, Patterns, and Deeper Questions
6. Make Collective Knowledge Visible

PRINCIPLE 1 — CREATE HOSPITABLE SPACE

Café hosts around the world emphasize the power and importance of creating a welcoming environment. Hospitable space means a safe and inviting space—a space where everyone feels comfortable to be themselves. A place where they can do their very best thinking, speaking and listening.

The Invitation: Creating hospitable space begins with the way you frame the invitation to participants. In your invitation, try to develop an initial *question* or *theme* (not a proposal or a problem) that you or your hosting group thinks those who are being invited really do care about. And make it a simple question or theme that creates curiosity and doesn't have a pat answer. Why have a conversation about something that doesn't really matter or to which you already have the answers in advance?

Let people know that this is not any ordinary conversation, but that it will be a café conversation—fun, engaging and creative. Everyone's contribution will make a difference to what will be discovered together in relation to the question—or to other questions that get raised as part of the conversation.

If you are sending out a written invitation, try to make it special in some way—informal, creative, colorful, and most important, with a personal touch. There's a difference between a business meeting and a café. A café conversation is about hospitality; conviviality and freedom—not formality and forced involvement.

The Physical Environment: What creates a comfortable space for a World Café conversation? The physical environment plays a large role in determining the success of your endeavor. While you may be convening several dozen or even several hundred people, it is essential to create an environment which evokes a feeling of informality and intimacy where people can feel comfortable.

If possible, make the space look like an actual café, with small round or square tables that seat four to five people. With fewer than four at a table there is often not enough diversity of perspectives, while more than five begins to limit the amount of personal interaction, making the café setting feel more like a meeting or a banquet.

Small round tables of 36 to 42 inches in diameter are ideal, but small card tables will work if round tables cannot be located. If tables are larger, they begin to act as barriers. Add colorful tablecloths (red and white checked is great), a candle or flowers. Put a couple of large white sheets of paper over the tablecloth and include pens and markers on each table to encourage scribbling, drawing, and connecting ideas. Easel sheets from flip chart pads work well. So do roll-ends of newsprint usually available from local newspaper printers. Or create placemats of letter or legal sized paper. What's important is that people can see each other's ideas (See Café Set Up and Supplies List at the end of this Guide).

Arrange the tables in a staggered, random fashion rather than in neat rows. Tables in a sidewalk café after it has been open for a few hours look relaxed, inviting and disarming. Try to create this type of café ambiance, even in a large meeting room. If it is difficult to set up an actual café environment, don't despair! There have been situations where it has been impossible to set up enough café tables for all the people who wanted to participate. You can easily modify the café design by scattering a few tables around the room to give it a café feeling. In a real pinch, you can omit café tables all together, although this limits the group's capacity to record its ideas on the tablecloth so everyone can see what's emerging.

If you are not using café tables or you are only using them for ambiance, create conversation clusters of 4-5 chairs placed in circles or crescents. When it is time for the conversation to begin, people can simply turn to one another and put their heads together around the question being posed. In addition, be sure to provide food or refreshments to honor our long traditions of community and hospitality. Whenever possible, add music, art, natural light, and plants. Use your imagination to create a welcoming and informal environment for your café gathering.

If you have a group of fewer than 12 participants, it is usually better to consider a dialogue circle, council, or other small group approach to fostering authentic conversation. The World Café is best suited to creating an hospitable space for connecting the intimacy of the small group with the excitement and fun of larger group participation and learning.

PRINCIPLE 2 — EXPLORE QUESTIONS THAT MATTER

People are reluctant to be in a conversation centered on things they don't care about. Finding and framing "questions that matter" to those who are coming to the café is an area where thought and attention can produce very profound results.

As people join in exploring questions they care about, they begin thinking together rather than spinning off into random directions. Well-crafted questions focus *intention*, attract *energy* and direct *attention* to what really counts. Suddenly the table comes alive with curiosity and excitement. Experienced café hosts tell us that open ended questions (the kind that don't have "yes" or "no" answers) work best. These questions need not imply immediate action steps or problem-solving. Instead, the questions should invite further inquiry and discovery.

For example, at a café in Denmark teachers, administrators, students and parents gathered to explore how they might improve their school system. The Café Host didn't settle on the more obvious question, "What problems do we have in our school?" Rather, he framed the question this way: "What could a good school also be?" In doing so, he opened the conversation to appreciating and exploring creative opportunities rather than limiting the group's attention to what wasn't working with the current situation.

Powerful Questions Focus Attention, Intention and Energy

What makes a powerful question? We have asked this of hundreds of people on several continents and several common themes have emerged.

A Powerful Question

- Is simple and clear
- Is thought-provoking
- Generates energy
- Focuses inquiry
- Challenges assumptions
- Opens new possibilities
- Evokes more questions

In some ways, World Café conversations are as much about discovering and exploring the right questions as they are about finding immediate answers. In café conversations collaborative learning, understanding, and insight are as important to creating positive results as formal planning or traditional problem solving.

Spend some time discovering and crafting the questions you want to use in your café. If possible, bounce them off key people who will be participating to see if the questions sustain interest and energy. If the event includes a speaker, involve that person in helping to create questions which, if explored, could make a difference to the real life concerns of those attending. You'll know you have a good question when it continues to surface new ideas and possibilities.

PRINCIPLE 3 — ENCOURAGE EACH PERSON'S CONTRIBUTION

Whether you are an overall café Host or the member of an individual table conversation, it is important to encourage everyone to contribute their ideas and perspectives, while allowing anyone who wants to contribute only through their listening or silent presence to do so. One of the reasons for having only four or five people at a café table or conversation cluster is to enable each voice to be heard. Often, people who are hesitant to speak in a large group have rich and exciting insights to offer in a more intimate café setting.

We find that people may feel freer to speak from the heart and listen more deeply to others if there is a *talking object* available to support the dialogue (it can be a stone, stick or any symbolic object—even a pen or salt shaker will do.) The use of a talking object has a long history. It was originally used by indigenous peoples to support courageous conversation, mutual respect, shared listening and wise decision-making. Each person at the table picks up the object when they are ready to speak or the talking object can move in a circle around the group. Another option is for the person who is holding the talking object to offer it as a gift to another member of their group when they have finished speaking. Of course, members have the opportunity to pass if they wish.

No one interrupts the person who is holding the talking object. Instead the other members listen attentively to the person speaking. Everyone listens for ideas, assumptions, perspectives and connections coming from that person's unique contribution. You might also encourage café members to allow a moment of silence between each person who speaks. This enables everyone a brief pause to reflect before adding their own thoughts.

At many Café gatherings, once the question is posed people are encouraged to simply jump into the conversation and begin to explore and share ideas. Often that's just what the group needs. As the Host, you can assess what combination of reflective listening through the use of a talking object, and exciting engagement through free flowing exchange will work the best.

PRINCIPLE 4 — CONNECT DIVERSE PEOPLE AND IDEAS

The opportunity to move between tables, meet new people, actively contribute your thinking and link the essence of your discoveries in ever widening circles is one of the distinguishing characteristics of the World Café's approach to dialogue and collaborative learning. This cross-pollination of people and ideas greatly enhances the richness of exchange and new insights. More perspectives surface and surprising combinations of insight and creativity often reveal themselves in ways people had not previously imagined.

Many Café hosts, after explaining the World Café Assumptions and Etiquette (included at the end of this Guide) set up three progressive rounds of conversation of approximately 20-30 minutes each. After several rounds of conversation, there is usually a period of sharing discoveries and insights in a town meeting-style conversation with the whole group.

Upon completing the initial round of conversation, one person agrees to remain at the table as the host while the others serve as travelers or "ambassadors of meaning." The travelers each go to new tables, carrying with them the core ideas, insights or deeper questions of their initial group. Café conversations might be described as akin to a progressive dinner party for collaborative inquiry, creative thinking and mutual discovery!

Ask the table host to welcome her new guests and share the high points of the initial conversation at that table. This can be done easily if you have encouraged the group to scribble or draw key ideas on the paper table cloth. Sometimes the members and the table host use large index cards or "placemats" in the middle of the table to note down key ideas to share with the travelers whom they will later welcome to their table.

As the travelers bring key insights or themes from their earlier conversations, ideas start to connect up to other ideas. Now the exploration spirals to another level. Often people will find a common theme in relation to the original question that takes them deeper. Or, someone will bring a counterpoint view or an unexpected connection that sparks a whole new avenue of relevant inquiry.

Like playing with Lego® blocks, we create new forms by using existing foundations and linking up additional unique combinations contributed by others. We describe this pattern of combining focus and freedom as "designing for emergence" or designing for "coherence without control." By the end of the second round, all of the tables or conversation clusters in the room will be pollinated with insights from prior conversations.

In the third round of conversation, people may return to their home (original) table to synthesize their discoveries, or continue traveling to new tables, leaving the same or a new host at the table. Sometimes a new question is posed for the third round of conversation that helps deepen the exploration.

At times, it is not the people who move, but their ideas. For example, as the Café Host, you can ask each person to write one key insight, idea or theme from the conversation they've been in and offer it as a gift to another table. Each member then exchanges their cards with a person from a nearby table. Each Café table reads the cards they've received aloud to provide creative input to a deepening round of conversation as it continues at their table.

Once you know what you want to achieve and the amount of time you have to work with, you can decide the appropriate number and length of conversation rounds, as well as the most interesting ways to connect and cross-pollinate ideas. Once you know the six principles that guide the World Café process, use your imagination to play, experiment and improvise.

PRINCIPLE 5 — LISTEN TOGETHER FOR PATTERNS, INSIGHTS AND DEEPER QUESTIONS

There is a word in Spanish called *El Meollo*. It means the essential nature or deeper substance of a thing. Members of World Café conversations often discover deeper patterns of meaning in what may appear, at first glance, to be a chaotic and messy exchange of ideas and perspectives.

In café conversations, it is important to emphasize *shared listening*—listening together for the collective wisdom or insight that no individual member of the group might have access to by themselves. As the overall Café Host, ask people to listen for new connections in the "space-in-between" what's being said. Encourage each Café table to take a bit of time for reflection during their inquiry together to notice "what's at the center of our conversation?"

As people enter the second round of sharing, remind participants to listen together for themes, discoveries or core questions that underlie the various emerging perspectives. At times a surprising flow of realizations or insights emerge as a result of this shared exploration. Everyone recognizes it as something special. One Scandinavian Café host calls this *"the magic in the middle."* These deeper discoveries may come at individual Café tables or later when the whole group harvests its collective insights.

At the end of the rounds of conversation, it is important, whenever possible, to engage in a *conversation of the whole.* These are not formal reports or analytical summaries. Rather, this time for mutual reflection offers the whole group an opportunity to discover the deeper themes or questions that are now present. Encourage a brief time of silence, and perhaps personal note-taking.

Focus attention during the reflection on what is most important for the group to explore at this stage. It is often in silence that a deeper intelligence or intuitive flash of new knowledge is revealed.

Ask anyone in the room to begin with key idea, theme or deeper question that has held real meaning for them. Then encourage others in the room to listen and notice what's been important from their own Café conversations that links to the contribution of the person sharing the initial idea. Imagine a ball of yarn passing overhead from one person in the room to another who shares a connected idea... and then to another and another. As the conversation continues, a new focus will likely emerge from somewhere else in the room. This person's contribution begins weaving additional threads to the collective tapestry of meaning.

Through practicing shared listening and placing disciplined attention on core themes, insights or questions we begin to develop a sense of connection to the larger whole. Mutual intelligence grows and evolves from linking individual contributions and perspectives that have been informed by multiple overlapping dialogues.

The purpose of the whole group conversation is not detailed data capture. That can happen by everyone contributing information on Post-Its or cards. Rather, it is an opportunity to become aware of the collaborative learning that has occurred and what has been especially meaningful or important to the members. Collective intelligence becomes more rich and accessible by paying mutual attention to levels of meaning and insight that may not have been visible at first glance.

PRINCIPLE 6 — MAKE COLLECTIVE KNOWLEDGE VISIBLE

Just by scribbling your ideas down on a napkin or a tablecloth, other Café members can literally see what you mean. Sometimes these are words. Sometimes they are pictures, shapes, or just colors. By writing and drawing, the group has created a shared space for weaving and connecting ideas at even deeper collective levels. There is something liberating about seeing your idea or insight placed on the paper in front of you and knowing that there is a memory of the key points being made. It also allows for a quick visual reference or reminder when reflecting together on what is emerging from the conversation.

In some Café events, a visual practitioner who uses words and pictures draws the group's ideas on a large wall mural as part of the whole group conversation. This allows everyone to see the relationships among key perspectives as well as the larger picture they are creating together. These colorful murals, often placed on a rolling blackboard or whiteboard, or on a flat wall on the side of the room, act like big tablecloths for the whole group.

At times, people will place their actual tablecloths on the wall and members will take a "gallery tour" of the group's ideas during a break. Or, at the end of a Café gathering, members can place large Post-Its with a single key insight per Post-It on a rolling white or blackboard or on the wall so that people can review the ideas during a break. This is a useful data gathering device for future planning. Sometimes volunteers can group this information so that clusters of related insights can be made visible and available for the group's next steps.

Some Cafés create a newspaper or a storybook to take the results of their work to larger audiences after the event. Create your own ways of making your group's collective knowledge and insights more visible. Whatever you do, participants will be able to deepen their collective understanding and make new connections as they literally *see* more of the whole.

THE ROLE OF THE OVERALL CAFÉ HOST AND THE TABLE HOST

The overall Café Host's job is to see that the six key World Café operating principles are put into action. It is not the specific form, but the embodiment of the principles that counts. This demands creativity, thoughtfulness, artistry and care. It's the Café Host who can make the difference between an interesting conversation and the magic of people accessing living knowledge and sources of deeper collective wisdom.

Neither the Café Host, nor the individual table host is actually a facilitator in the traditional sense, since World Café conversations are largely self-managing and self-organizing. In fact, we've found that having formal facilitators at individual tables tends to reduce the effectiveness and excitement of the Café experience. What's important is not formal facilitation at small tables, but rather the thoughtful setup of the overall Café environment, clear instructions regarding Café etiquette and logistics, management of time in a gentle way, and the capacity to harvest, weave and connect ideas in the town meeting portions of the Café.

The role of the overall Café Host is to:

- Help frame the invitation
- Work with others to create an hospitable, welcoming and informal Café Environment
- Welcome the participants
- Tell people the purpose of the gathering
- Pose the question or theme for rounds of conversation—and make sure that the question is visible to everyone either on an overhead, on cards at the tables or on an easel sheet
- Provide the few simple World Café guidelines (See Café Assumptions and Café Etiquette under Materials for Café Hosting at the end of this Resource Guide)—often on an overhead projector or an easel sheet
- Tell people how the logistics of the Café will work, including the role of the table host, who will be asked to volunteer to stay at the end of the first round

- Move among the tables, being available to encourage everyone's voice to be included, to remind people to jot down key ideas, doodle and draw and to answer questions, if requested
- Help keep the time for the rounds of conversation in a gentle and nonintrusive way. Raising your hand quietly, and encouraging other people to do the same when they notice yours raised can be a signal to wind down their table conversations and prepare for the next round
- Host the conversations of the whole
- Make sure that key insights are recorded visually or are gathered and posted if at all possible
- Be creative in adapting the six Café operating principles to meet the unique needs of your own situation.\

The Role of the Table Host is to:

- Help jot down or draw (along with others at the table) key connections, insights, discoveries and deeper questions as they emerge
- Stay behind to welcome the travelers from other tables
- Briefly share the key insights from the prior Café conversation so others can link and build using ideas from their respective conversations

Is the World Café More Than Just Talk?

We, as humans, have the unique capacity for reflection and making meaning together. As meaning changes for us, so does our way of being and acting in the world. As we share our stories and ideas with each other in a welcoming environment, our sense of possibilities and creative opportunities can undergo subtle and occasionally profound changes.

People who have used the World Café to explore important questions usually find that participants are challenged in new ways. When a conversation comes alive, people naturally gravitate to considering possibilities for action—both individually and collectively. Collaborative conversation is "real work" and World Café conversations often lead to powerful outcomes. When people come to a new level of shared understanding around real-life issues, they usually want to make a difference. And when participants build on one another's knowledge, they will most likely see action choices they didn't even know existed before.

There is nothing more powerful than a community engaged in conversation in relation to what it cares about. Pull up a chair. Sit down and talk. Listen and build on what you learn. Host a World Café conversation yourself. You might be surprised at what emerges!

Where to Go for Additional Information

Like the World Café process itself, this Guide is evolving. As you experiment with hosting your own World Café Conversations we'd love to hear from you, both about your Café experiences and about ways we can make this Resource Guide even more useful. Contact ken@theworldcafe.com with ideas and feedback. And for further detailed background information, including World Cafe stories, additional hosting tips, supporting articles, and links to related Café and dialogue initiatives, please visit http://www.theworldcafe.com

MATERIALS TO SUPPORT CAFÉ HOSTING

Assumptions Underlying World Café Conversations

- The knowledge and wisdom we need is already present & accessible
- Collective insight evolves from...
  - Honoring unique contributions
  - Connecting ideas
  - Listening into the middle
  - Noticing deeper themes and questions
- Intelligence emerges as the system connects to itself in diverse and creative ways

Café Etiquette

- **Focus** on what matters
- **Contribute** your thinking and experience
- **Speak** from the heart
- **Listen** to understand
- **Link and Connect** ideas
- **Listen Together** for deeper themes, insights and questions
- **Play, Doodle, Draw**—writing on the tablecloths is encouraged!

Room Set Up

(*Note: The room set up is described for an ideal situation. Your venue may not fit this model exactly. Don't panic. You can create a great World Café by using your imagination to improvise and design the unique way in which your Café reflects the six basic operating principles—with or without red checkered tablecloths!*)

- A room with natural light and view to outside foliage, if at all possible. If not, try to put plants or flowers around the room to give the Café a natural feeling.
- Flat wall space to put mural paper or table cloths on one side of the room or two large rolling white boards, if you have a visual practitioner for your Café.
- Small round or square tables (approx. 36 inches to 42 inches in diameter) that can seat 4 or 5. Card tables work as well, although round tables tend to create more of a Café ambiance

- Room size large enough so that people can comfortably move among the tables and so that the Café Host can move among the tables without disturbing seated participants
- Tables spread in a slightly chaotic fashion (not in rows—a random distribution around the room)
- Checkered tablecloths or other informal color tablecloths. If none exist, then white tablecloths will work. Even just putting pieces of easel or flip chart paper on the table will work
- Two pieces of white flip chart paper on each table (like in a café where people write on the table cloths)
- One wine glass or other small glass on each table that can hold several different colored Crayola or other felt tipped pens
- Crayola, Mr. Sketch or other water based felt tipped pens in several different colors (red, green, blue, black—the kind you buy for children in the plastic packs—enough for each group of 4 participants to have several colors on each table (placed in the glasses on each table)
- One small vase with sprigs of fresh (not plastic) flowers on each table and/or one votive candle
- One Café table set up to put presenter and/or Host's materials on at front of the room
- Coffee, tea, and refreshments for participants. Water and glasses in the room.
- Enough chairs for all participants and presenters (with capacity to remove extra chairs)

Equipment and Supplies

(Note: these are optional depending on the size of the group and the purpose of your Café)

- Overhead projector and screen and table large enough to hold overheads
- A sound system that can play both tapes and CDs with good speakers for music
- Microphones for Café hosts or speakers—2 wireless lavalier (if needed, depending on number of participants) and two handheld wireless mikes for town meeting-style sessions
- 4 flip charts with blank white flip chart paper
- Two 4x6 or 4x8 rolling white boards or blackboards

- A supply box which contains basic supplies (stapler, paper clips, rubber bands, markers, 1 masking tape, pens, pushpins, pencils and post-it pads)
- Extra pens for participants
- Colored 4x6 or 5x8 cards in any color other than white—enough for each participant to have what they may need for personal note taking as they move from table to table (if you choose for them to do this since they may not bring their own paper)
- 4 x 6 large stickies (Post-Its) in bright colors—divided in small packs of 25 stickies—one package for each table (if you are using them for people to write ideas and post them)

COMMUNITY ORGANIZING

Description: Community Organizing is a process of development which was created for and primarily used in the political and social sphere of American life. Its main emphasis is on finding and empowering leaders at a grassroots level to knit together coalitions around different issues of justice and progress in society. The tools perfected by the originators of Community Organizing can be used in congregational development as well and, because of the emphasis which is laid on developing leaders from all areas and strata of life, these are especially conducive to Mutual Ministry efforts. The understanding of the nature of power and the redefinition of leadership which Community Organizing promotes also helps in visualizing (and therefore following through on) the basic principles of democratic action.

Format: Community Organizing uses the technique of having an "organizer" target people in the local community who have the capacity to empower and work with others. These potential leaders are then invited to gather and learn the principles of democratic action. Workshops are a mixture of theory and practice geared to equipping these leaders with the tools they need to knit together their community to take action on some issue which is of pressing concern to them. They learn to work together as a team to accomplish goals they set themselves.

The four main "tools" of Community Organizing are relational meetings, house meetings, research actions and general assemblies. With these tools, the leaders prepare the community to exercise power, i.e. to act. Some of these tools have been mentioned in the first section as helpful in a number of different situations. The whole process of Community Organizing, though, can be used as a method of congregational development.

Indications for use: In my experience, the church which chooses Community Organizing as their development program will be successful if they have enough people (at least 50), a strong sense of identity and purpose and an organizer who can spend at least a year leading them through the process.

The two tools (relational meetings and house meetings) which can also be used in conjunction with other methods will be described below in greater detail.

Cautions: To do Community Organizing well takes great commitment to changing the culture of the congregation, but provides no way to ease into this. Therefore, if the church community lacks self-confidence or has a rector/pastor who is not ready to change his or her place in the traditional hierarchy, the effort will be ineffectual as a congregational development effort (although many churches use this as a foundation for outreach ministry).

When using Community Organizing as a development program, it is also important to have an organizer who is focused on the congregation, rather than on gleaning leadership for a wider community effort. I believe a church which has gone through this process will provide more leadership in the outside community after it has undergone the effort internally, but the goal of developing the church community needs to be the initial priority.

More information: While there are many books on Community Organizing, there is no better way to learn the basics than by getting training from one of the well-known groups such as Industrial Area Fellowship (IAF). Some denominations, such as the Evangelical Lutheran Church of America, are promoting Community Organizing at a national level and may offer instruction. Partnering with a trained Community Organizer who is committed to the work of the congregation may also be a possibility.

On the pages following, I offer the story of a congregation where I was rector, and how we partnered with an Episcopal priest, who was also an organizer, to do congregational development.

See also sections on redefining power and leadership, relational meetings, and house meetings.

Finding and Developing Leaders in a Neighborhood Church

(Using principles of Community Organizing)

THE EPISCOPAL CHURCH OF ST. MATTHEW

TUCSON, ARIZONA

2000

Abstract: As the result of a training process developed by the Industrial Areas Foundation (IAF), primarily emphasizing and developing leadership, 27 new and renewed leaders were developed at St. Matthew's Episcopal Church, Tucson, AZ over a nine-month training process. St. Matthews is a large pastoral size congregation with approximately 175 members worshipping on Sunday mornings. There is one clergy staff person.

by The Rev. Margaret A. Babcock
and The Rev. Paul Buckwalter

WHY WE DID IT

It is often said (so often that it must surely be in the public domain) that the definition of "crazy" is doing the same thing over and over again… yet expecting new and different results each time. The church community seems especially vulnerable to this kind of madness as it tries to hold onto its rich and treasured past while seeking a path into future that is unpredictable and uncharted. At St. Matthew's Episcopal Church in Tucson, AZ the question was never whether we would work towards solutions, but how we could find new ways to approach our problems as we came to realize that we were working harder and harder while making less and less progress with the tried and true methods we knew.

The issue we wanted to tackle was that of leadership: Given who we were and the resources available to us, how could we find the energetic leadership we needed to carry out the ministry we felt called to do? We knew that volunteer lay ministers were tired and the rector was overworked. We knew that financially we would not be able to hire a second priest, even part-time, in the near future. Repeated articles in the newsletter encouraging people to help, inspiring sermons about the responsibility of all baptized members to take their place in ministry, pleas in the bulletin and sign-up sheets in the narthex did little to increase volunteers or energize existing leadership. Out of desperation (the mother of all true change) we opted to hire a priest, who also happened to be a community organizer, to be our consultant and teach us the IAF (Industrial Areas Foundation) method of leadership development. The Rev. Paul Buckwalter joined us in January of 2000 with a contract to be present two Sundays a month and work with the rector and a team of likely leaders for nine months. This is the story of that experiment.

WHO WE WERE

St. Matthew's entered the new millennium as a parish which knew itself well. 150-200 members attended church on Sunday, putting it on the boundary between the pastoral and program=sized church, where it had been teetering since 1991. Paid staff included a full-time rector, part-time office manager, and part-time music director. Since 1996, we had been in a process of self-discernment and goal setting. The rector had developed a workshop designed to help members discover and articulate the basic personality of a congregation and different leaders of the parish had been involved in three of these meetings. The portrait which emerged was of a "Servant" congregation connected to its neighborhood. At heart, this parish was very personal, enjoying helping ministries on a one to one basis. It also, however, showed a passion for the larger plights of children and the elderly and was feeling a call to reach beyond its immediate boundaries to engage the larger world. And finally, its identity as an Episcopal church, representing a minority expression of the Christian faith in this middle class part of town, was clearly central to the personality of St. Matthew's.

Once the leadership and members had a chance to reflect on who they were as a congregation, the next step was to grapple with who they felt called by God to become.

While many were happy with the portrait they saw, most realized that it was not an option to stay static. The problem with just envisioning and planning is that is usually doesn't provide energy to move forward unless actions are taken. Growth in spirit and numbers was needed to keep the community vital. Focus groups were formed to discuss the issues of values and dreams and in 1998 the vestry took all the information gathered in these groups and formulated a mission statement, motto and a set of three-year goals. When they came back together in 1999, the vestry reviewed and revised the goals. It was clear that while much work had been done, leader burnout was high and the parish as a whole was not growing. This was the context into which the concept of community organizing was introduced.

WHAT WE DID

The outline of the basic process introducing St. Matthews to community organization was put together by the rector (The Rev. Margaret A. Babcock) and the priest-consultant (The Rev. Paul Buckwalter) as a way to address immediate needs in the parish as well as to initiate this new dimension in congregational life. Because leader burnout was high and the rector was overburdened, it was decided that most of the meetings would take place on Sundays when people were already gathered and the consultant could be present at worship to assist and preach once a month. This turned out to be a fortunate decision which was foundational to the success of the work.

Even before the contract of 20 days' work began in January of 2000, the consultant met with the rector to teach her the fundamentals of the relational meetings and definitions of the three kinds of leaders. He then sent her out to find 10-12 primary leaders who would form the Kitchen Cabinet Leadership team. The Leadership and Development project was to last nine months, from January through October. Primary leaders were asked to join with the understanding that there would be a definite break point at the end of the nine months, with the option to re-enlist or expand the group. The Kitchen Cabinet met with the rector and the consultant after Sunday services twice a month for two hours to learn the skills of relationship building inside the parish and also in the wider community.

On the first Sunday that the consultant was present, he preached to the whole congregation at each service and set forth a theology of relationship culture and relationship building. In subsequent sermons he expanded on these topics and engaged conversationally with the congregation in sermons on relationship and community building. The Annual Meeting of the parish was in January, at which time the rector was able to review what the congregation had discovered about themselves in previous years, frame the issues the church was grappling with and invite the support of the whole community for this new effort.

Throughout January and February, the work centered on teaching and practicing "one on one" relational meetings between the leadership team and members of the congregation. The IAF concept of three levels of leadership was explained and discussed. Reviews were held at the meetings after church. The Kitchen Cabinet members had a chance to share and critique their efforts, as well as give the rector feedback on parishioners and their potential for leadership. In March, the team began to learn about and plan for house meetings, a series of four to be held in May and June for parishioners. The consultant also put together an interim report on the state of the parish, which was subsequently shared with the vestry and proved helpful in getting the elected policy leaders on board with the leadership project.

Planning and rehearsal for the house meetings, as well as further relationship meetings, took up the April meetings. Throughout April, recruiting for the house meetings was going on. There was some confusion as to the purpose of these meetings, as well as some resistance on the part of long-time members who saw them as similar to focus group which had already been done. The topic of discussion being raised at the first two meetings was internal: "What Gives Life to St. Matthews: Spiritual Journeys" and for the second two, external: "Our Mission and Service to the World." Attendance at the meetings was between 20 and 30 participants. The house meetings afforded an entrance point for some new members of the parish and gave the opportunity to voice concerns for more longtime members. We adjusted our plan to fit the interest by dropping the fourth meeting.

While the house meetings were being held we began talking about doing relational meetings with people in the outside community. The Kitchen Cabinet collaborated with the consultant about who might be interviewed and a list was drawn up of community leaders in the local IAF organization as well as the mayor, city council members, and school principals. Kitchen Cabinet members were assigned in pairs to meet with these people and given the summer to complete the task.

In June, Kitchen Cabinet members turned their attention to the planning of three workshops to be held in August and September. The purpose of these workshops was to gather the leadership of the parish, especially the participants from the relational meetings, those at the house meetings, and the traditional leaders (vestry and chairs of committees) in order to look in greater depth at what action steps the whole parish could take in three areas: Evangelism, Liturgy and Music, and Extended Ministry. This organizing activity was done to prepare our leadership for an all-parish General Assembly on St. Matthew's Day in September. New leaders were drawn in to help plan the workshops. Leadership teams were formed and assignments given out at the end of June. When the all-day workshops took place at the end of August and early in September, they were attended by 18-25 people each.

The General Assembly was, in IAF terms, "doing an action on the parish." It was scheduled for the patron saint's day, the last Sunday in September, and was planned around worship, so that after the assembly all members would be together in celebration of their faith to engage with this action. Normally, there are three service at St. Matthew's on Sunday, but this day there was only one. The leaders, who emerged from the workshops, came together to rehearse their presentations on the Thursday before the assembly.

At the General Assembly, the rector initially framed the event by providing an overview of the parish and its journey, describing the challenge of our time in a new metaphor that evolved out of the nine-month process. The Senior Warden then reviewed the history of the leadership project and the process that we had been working with since January. The leaders of the three workshops then reported their action recommendations. We asked for a response from the congregation by having them turn to their neighbors and share what they had heard and what they had found interesting or exciting in these recommendations. Three parishioners were then asked to share what they were talking about to the group as a whole. The Senior Warden (chair of the parish board or vestry) raised implications for the budget and the rector wrapped up with a look to the future.

In the month after the General Assembly, the Kitchen Cabinet took some time to evaluate both the General Assembly and the process they had been through in the past year. The rector asked the members to consider staying on as Kitchen Cabinet members and to meet monthly with the vestry as a way to focus the work of the parish, as well as continue doing relational meetings, especially with new people. Task forces out of the three workshops also began meeting and planning to begin work towards the goals they had set.

WHAT WE LEARNED

In the evaluations, it was clear that we all felt that we had indeed done something different and valuable… but what exactly had we learned about the process?

1) **The IAF process of leadership development is effective in a mid-sized, middle class, Episcopal Church.** A leadership core of 10 people was activated to organize the congregation and 27 people came forward to commit to leadership roles in the parish. They pledged themselves to this work in front of the whole congregation. Several of these leaders were new to the parish or had not taken high profile positions before. There was a good diversity between the old guard and newer members and the membership of all three worship services was represented. 6 men and 21 women made these commitments.

2) **The Rector (Senior Pastor) needs to make leadership development his or her primary responsibility for the life of the parish.** It was evident to all of us involved that the leadership development process through the nine-month period outlined above was invasive to the whole culture of the parish. If the parish is primarily pastoral or client-oriented, this kind of new direction not only changes program but shifts the whole mission of the community. The rector or senior pastor, therefore, needs to make an upfront decision to put other responsibilities and duties after his or her commitment to the leadership development process. Otherwise, the culture of the parish will remain the same and the pastor's work will most likely remain reactive rather than proactive.

3) **It was very important to build the leadership process around and into the worship of the congregation.** It became evident that the presence of the priest consultant at services was integral to the message that this process is relationship-based and not issue-driven. Worship is where the central relationship of the community, our covenant with God, is expressed, rejoiced in, and challenged to grow. The members of the congregation were regularly invited to reflect on how their relationship with God called them into relationship with others… not only in the congregation but in the wider community. The presence of the rector at Sunday morning worship regularly pointing to the new way of life for the community was critical. The leaders of the Kitchen Cabinet were constantly acknowledged as they were publicly called into meetings and so easily recognized by other members who wanted to be in conversation with them. It was evident to all that a reconfiguration of power was taking place publicly, constantly and steadily. All members had the opportunity engage in this dynamic at some level throughout the year.

4) **The three-tier leadership model, while helpful in identifying the capacity of leaders, needed to be reframed for congregational life.** The titles of the leadership types, i.e. Primary, Secondary, and Tertiary, were renamed Red, Yellow, and Blue to avoid perpetuating the hierarchical idea that some kinds of leaders are more valuable than others. There was a recognition that instead of just looking for primary or red leaders, we encouraged finding leaders in all categories. IAF methodology for finding leaders and types of leaders works somewhat differently inside a congregation than in a community organization. A community organization is an open political system which puts priority on finding and developing primary (red) leadership, while acknowledging that secondary (yellow) and tertiary (blue) leadership can and do serve as feeding grounds for the development of primary leaders. Community organizers ordinarily are not looking for yellow and blue leaders, who tend to be issue and task oriented rather than being focused on power and developing the community organization.

   I.   Parishes are in many ways closed systems. While the training of leaders is still centered on primary (red) leaders, it is also necessary to be more inclusive by searching for secondary (yellow) and tertiary (blue) leaders as well. This is because much of the mission driving a congregation is issue-oriented, task-directed, and program-based. Raising up all three types of leadership and acknowledging them in worship each Sunday morning is important for the empowerment of the whole community.

II.   It is important that the call to leadership be based on the priesthood of all believers and on our call to responsibly offer our gifts, as varied as they are, to God's service. Biblical stories, particularly those of Moses, Jesus, and Paul, and their use of leadership are important in conveying this theme and should be referred to constantly during the training process.

5) **Power Analysis of the parish and the community is critical both during the training and after the General Assembly.** Early in the training process, consultants and organizers need to teach an understanding of power and do a power analysis of the parish. When the community relational meetings begin, a power analysis of the community should be done.

6) **Timelines for the Leadership Development Project** --- While most of the Kitchen Cabinet members felt that the nine months of twice monthly meetings were adequate for the training, there was acknowledgment that the participation and commitment of the group fell off significantly during late May, June and July. The lack of interest in House Meetings was to a great extent attributed to holding them in May and June, and we were criticized for meeting when our "winter visitor" population was gone and our school-age families were on vacation. Perhaps planning to take a summer break would have been helpful, although that would have broken the momentum of the process and put the General Assembly in December, raising issues around the level of Christmas activity and liturgical stress. The best alternative suggested was that the process should start in September and end in May…leaving the summer as a natural time to regroup.

7) **Relational Meetings worked!** The Kitchen Cabinet conducted approximately 35-40 relational meetings in the parish and 18-20 with community leaders. The results were deepened connections with parishioners, the identification and recruitment of leaders, and the beginnings of institutional connections with power leaders in the city.

CONCLUSION

Overall, the IAF model of leadership identification and training gave St. Matthews a method for increasing the leadership energy in our own congregation. It also shifted the focus from the rector as main instigator of ministry to lay leaders who are now willing not only to take on parish issues but engage structures and institutions in the community as well. The task for the future is to continually update the leadership process by a commitment to continuing the relational meetings and to holding house meetings on a regular basis. We have found a new and effective way of being the Church. Time will tell if it is sustainable.

DEFINITIONS

Relational Meetings (also known as one-on-ones): A brief (30-45 minute) interaction with someone to determine what motivates and inspires them, what their self-interest is and where you have points of mutual interest.

House Meetings: Groups of 6-10 people led in a focused discussion by one or two leaders in order to find leaders in an organization or parish.

Workshops/Retreats: Groups of 18-25 people who are led by a leadership team in exploring issues of common interest and setting goals for the larger institution.

Leaders: The IAF model designates three types of leaders (primary, secondary and tertiary) all of which generate followers. In summary, the Primary (Red) leaders have a sense of vision about the institution or parish and are interested in power and how it is used. These leaders want to grow personally, and are invested in finding and developing other leaders for the organization. Secondary (Yellow) leaders focus their energies on programs, projects or issues. Tertiary (Blue) leaders focus their skills on "hands on" activities.

COMMUNITY ORGANIZING:
REDEFINING POWER AND LEADERSHIP

Description: Changing the mental models of at least a critical mass of people in the congregation is imperative if a movement of equal partnership is to be sustained. The best challenge I have found to our societal norms around the subjects of power and leadership has been an introduction to Community Organizing and its definitions of these concepts. Any conversational exercises can be utilized to frame such dialogue. However, usually different definitions need to be laid out so that people see there are truly options for how we think about these words and how those options may open up new ways of relating to each other.

Format: I usually introduce conversation about power and leadership at the beginning of a congregational development effort, inviting people to consider what their theology says about these concepts. It is important to hear and take seriously what people are thinking. (I find when participants begin to articulate what they think about power and leadership it's usually a mixed bag with lots of different experiences, both negative and positive.) A period of Bible study on the issue of power may also prove helpful in limbering up critical faculties for deep dialogue. After exploring what the current and biblical definitions seem to be, it's time to lay out the Community Organizing definitions for consideration.

If you have been trained in the IAF (Industrial Areas Foundation) method of Community Organizing, you will notice that I have modified the names of the leadership styles. I have tried to modify the vertically hierarchical methodology created in the IAF (Primary, Secondary and Tertiary leaders) and replaced it with a more democratic metaphor (Red, Yellow and Blue leaders). Not only does this validate the equality of these leadership styles, but it allows us to consider how styles may be blended in individuals, like primary colors combine, to get variations. (Many thanks to the Rev Paul Buckwalter who developed the first iteration of this way of looking at leadership style in our work in Tucson, AZ.)

In church work, all kinds of leaders are needed and must be cultivated. Organizers working in the Church, unlike political organizers, have a responsibility to empower all members to be ministers. Understanding the native style and also the potential of members is an invaluable asset when doing discernment for ministry roles.

Indications for Use: It is imperative to replace the mental model of a vertically hierarchical community with a model of shared partnership, if development in a Mutual Ministry model is to be sustained. An early weakness of the Mutual Ministry model was that it did not fully articulate and encourage this systemic shift. Conversations about different ways to embody both power and leadership are necessary to vital Mutual Ministry congregations.

Cautions: To truly be incorporated into the culture of a church, new definitions cannot be imposed. Instead, they need to be discovered as relevant and helpful by the members. Continued support needs to be given so new mental models are retained against the inevitable societal pressure to revert to older, hierarchical models. The bottom line is: If you aren't ready to keep having this conversation for at least five years, you may not be ready to engage in Mutual Ministry. That said, there is no better time to begin than now. And this is a very good place to begin!

Directions: On the following pages are notes and handouts to start a conversation about power and leadership.

REDEFINING "POWER"

Community Organizing Motto: "Power Precedes Program"

Power must <u>always</u> precede program... This is very important, because we often think that if we just get hold of the right program we'll be able to get people involved. But that's like buying the most expensive car in the world without checking to see if you have a source for gas! It doesn't matter if you think the project of participating in feeding the hungry is the greatest thing since sliced bread. It doesn't even matter if your outreach committee has come up with some pretty great ideas.

If you haven't organized for power internally, those projects and the understanding of Mission they represent will die out when the people doing them burnout (and they will burn out if they don't have real and deep congregational support). Better to drill for oil first and then have enough gas to drive a scooter, than to have a Humvee that can't get out of the driveway! Not having gas (power) is what most people complain about, especially when invited into Mutual Ministry. What are all the excuses? We're too old. We don't have enough members. We don't have enough time. Building power before expending it deals with these complaints.

POWER = ABILITY, CAPACITY AND WILLINGNESS TO ACT

- Definition: In community organizing power is understood as the ability, capacity and willingness to act. We can understand this as an individual's power... but we also can look at this as a group's ability, capacity, and willingness.

- Power does have different sources and the kind of power we want to build for Mutual Ministry is "Relational" power (power with) as defined by Community Organizing. (This as opposed to hierarchical or "power over"). Explore the concept of "power over" vs "power with" by having a conversation about the polarity between the two.

POWER OVER VS. POWER WITH

Power = ability, capacity and willingness to act, but we experience different kinds of power.

POWER OVER	**POWER WITH**
(World as is)	(World as it should be)
Dominant	Relational
Control	Interaction
Unilateral	Fair
One-way communication	Communication as dialogue
Status/Hierarchy	Collective/Participation
Private/closed groups	Public/open
Not accountable	Accountable and transparent

What are examples of both kinds of power in your congregation? In the community? Where is the formal power in your congregation? Informal power? How does this work back and forth?

REDEFINING LEADERSHIP

What is a leader?

Hierarchical definition: The one who has the vision.

Community Organizing definition: Anyone who brings another to the table for negotiation, conversation and visioning.

Mutual Ministry definition: Anyone who brings another to the Lord's Table for all of the above plus nurture and partnership with God.

LEADERSHIP CHARACTERISTICS

While we often look for such qualities as self-sufficiency and expertise in hierarchical leadership, Community Organizing asks us to look at a different set of characteristics as we assess the level of competence in leaders. Remember, the goal is not to manipulate people to do what the leader wants... it is rather to bring people along to share their perspective, gifts, and talents at the common table. So, what these characteristics show us is a level of spiritual health that will be the foundation of any good leader.

LEADERSHIP CHARACTERISTICS

1. Anger -- in touch with one's anger and able to use it productively

2. Humor -- the antidote to anger, if one can laugh at one's self

3. Curiosity

4. Understanding death -- acquainted with human limitations

5. Imagination

6. Hope

7. Objectivity

8. Risk Taker -- not taking unreasonable risks, but letting one's feet leave the ground at times

9. Clear on self-interest

LEADERSHIP TYPES

After being clear about what characteristics we are looking for, community organizing recognizes three different types of leaders. All types of leaders are needed in the church. If any of these types is missing, the community is going to need a lot of help to mature. A disclaimer: People are more complicated than theories. No one fits perfectly into any of these categories…and most of us will move into different modes of leadership at different times in our lives.

Red Leaders: These are the people who see the whole forest and appreciate how the trees fit together. Often called bridge builders, these are leaders you want to help organize whole communities and serve on ministry support teams, vestries, etc. They are often not appreciated by rectors and pastors who may see them as a threat.

Some things to listen for if you think you might be talking to a red leader:

> ➤ Interest in personal development
>
> ➤ Self-respect
>
> ➤ Clarity around their own values and vision
>
> ➤ Not issue-centered
>
> ➤ Concerned with the development of leaders
>
> ➤ Reflective and able to suffer
>
> ➤ Capacity to compromise
>
> ➤ In touch with anger and humor
>
> ➤ Interested in power (action)

Yellow Leaders: These are people who are particularly attracted to and bonded with one kind of tree in the forest, i.e. one program or population. Often they are very effective in their area of interest and therefore are asked to take on red leader responsibilities. They tend to be exclusive in their focus, though, and therefore not as invested in bringing people with differing interests together.

If you are listening to a yellow leader, you might hear:

> ➤ Great concern about a particular issue
>
> ➤ Looking for power… for self and issue
>
> ➤ Wanting recognition (about area of interest)
>
> ➤ Understanding of the difference between activity and action (i.e. activity is a task and action will lead to transformation)
>
> ➤ Strategic thinking

Blue Leaders: These leaders are lone tree people, who rarely think of themselves as leaders. They are, however, very effective in our Community Organizing/Mutual Ministry definitions of leadership, bringing other people to the table one at a time. Maybe because of this style, they are often the most effective evangelists, making and bringing friends into community. These leaders may be "guilted" into being on the governing boards or other committees... but will be miserable. They much prefer to have a task that they can work on and invite others to help with, to meeting where they have to plan with others.

In conversing with a blue leader, you may be aware they:

- ➢ Use personal talent

- ➢ Invite others to use their talents

- ➢ Respond to jobs which need to be done

- ➢ Think of themselves as volunteers

- ➢ Make good project managers

COMMUNITY ORGANIZING:
RELATIONAL MEETINGS

Description: The foundational tool of Community Organizing is the relational meeting, which allows organizers to get to know people at the level of their motivations and expedites identification of personal leadership styles. These 30-45 minute meetings take place between an organizer and one other person, with the organizer asking questions which direct the speaker to offer a deeper level of his or her story than normally imparted at coffee hours or cocktail parties.

The goal of these encounters is three-fold: First, the organizer listens for shared points of energy or interest, thereby building the potential for power in the community. Second, the listener is curious about what motivates this speaker, and what actions he or she might be interested in connecting and helping with in the future. Finally, the organizer is evaluating what style of leadership this person has or may be capable of.

Format: There are three distinct phases of a relational meeting:

1. The first step is to plan. Depending on the situation, this consists of deciding who you will have relational meetings with (either by your own choice or coordinating with a team which is doing these meetings) and then contacting those people, getting an agreement about when and for how long to meet.
2. The next step is to act. This means having the meeting and asking directive questions while listening intently.
3. The final step is to evaluate, recording what you have learned about the person you were talking with and sharing appropriate insights with your team (if you are working with others).

Indications for Use: In the full form of Community Organizing, relational meetings are used to get to know the people who will be the body of the organization. This tool allows organizers to quickly connect those they talk with to others who share motivations and invite them into roles which will best utilize their gifts for leadership.

Relational meetings are also used to connect with community leaders and help build bridges between different groups in the community. It is an invaluable method of discovering what truly interests a community leader, such as a mayor or school principal. Knowing the motivations of such leaders helps organizers build the power they need to get things accomplished.

Other less traditional uses of relational meetings include community building within a congregation where members don't really know each other at a deep level. It is a tool which helps build partnership between members as they learn to listen deeply to each other. It also is useful at the time of gifts assessment, to determine what kind of leadership style and skills individuals in the church have and where their deepest motivation (and hence greatest energy for service and ministry) lies.

Another important benefit of training and practicing relational meetings together is that participants begin to think and act as a team which has as its core value the empowerment of all people. This is the kind of team which will do congregational development in a Mutual Ministry style quite naturally. If nothing else, you might consider relational meetings as a way to knit together your core group of developers into a partnership.

Cautions: While simple to learn and easy to use, a sense of not wanting to be exposed to rejection can make people reluctant to commit to this exercise. Most groups require support when initiating a course of relational meetings. People need not only instruction, but practice with others who are "safe" (like members of their team or trusted friends), before they venture out to talk to less well-known members, or even community leaders who may not belong to the church.

It is tempting to expect too much too soon after training people in the art of relational meetings. If you use this tool, be sure you have support and regular check-ins scheduled for your organizers.

Directions: Following are two exercises from the "Rooted in God" program that can be used to teach relational meetings. The first is a warm-up exercise and the second gives the basics of training to use this tool.

WARM-UP EXERCISE FOR RELATIONAL MEETINGS[56]

Activity   *Session Leader*   **20 minutes**

Divide into groups of three. Each member in the small groups takes a turn at telling a story from their life in one of the following areas:

1. Epiphany (an "Aha!" experience) or

2. Sickness unto death (physical, mental or spiritual) or

3. Conversion (a turn-around experience)

Discussion (Plenary)   *Session Leader*   **15 minutes**

* How did it feel to share?

* Any places where stories intersected?

* What was particularly interesting?

Note: *Power to transform comes from sharing stories: My story/Your story=Our story (throw in God's story and you really have power!)

Evaluation   *Session Leader*   **10 minutes**

* How did this go for you tonight?

* Any insights, concerns, questions?

TRAINING FOR RELATIONAL MEETINGS[57]

| Discussion | Session Leader | 15 minutes |

Read together the following explanation of **Relationship Meetings,** and go over the handouts provided. If you would like to read more about Community Organizing and the tools it offers for building relational power, a good book to start with is *Transforming Power: Biblical Strategies for Making a Difference in Your Community* by Robert Linthicum, Intervarsity Press, ©2003.

> Explanation of Relationship Meetings: In the last session we discovered how much energy is generated in sharing our deep stories of transformation, epiphany and sickness unto death. To know the people of our community at this level is to tap into great potential for transformation. But how can we get to know people at this level, without seeming pushy or manipulative?

In Community Organizing, one way relational power is built is through the exercise of "relationship meetings". A relationship meeting is a 30-45 minute session between two people, where one person asks thoughtful questions which get beneath the surface of another person's history to find that person's real story and the places where they can connect. The intention is to establish a relationship with that person at the level of the interests, issues and passions this person has energy around. (*Go over the handout on "What a Relationship Meeting Is/Is Not About".*) The questioner will want to explore in some depth the kinds of subjects that are shown on the second handout...but don't feel like you have to explore each of these subjects in one sitting! (*Look at the handout entitled "Relationship Meeting Subjects".*)

How does one do a relationship meeting? There are three stages if this intentional building of relational power is to be successful:

1 — Plan:

Think carefully about who you want to do such a meeting with, and then call the person to set up a time. You may say something like, "I'm a member of the *Rooted in God* program and we are talking about how to get to know other members of our congregation. I thought it would be interesting to get to know you more and would like 30-45 minutes of your time just to sit down and talk. Would you be willing to meet me for coffee after the service next Sunday?"

2 —Act:

Meet your appointment promptly and begin with a general question. Something like "How did you come to join this church?" or "Tell me about what you do when you are not in church," will get the ball rolling. Then, as the discussion progresses, don't be afraid to interrupt to ask deeper questions when a subject that catches your interest comes up. For example, if a person is talking about her history and mentions that she was once a Girl Scout leader, you might want to stop her recitation, mention that you had once been a Girl Scout and ask what motivated her to work with girls in this way. Be sure to end the conversation when you said you would and indicate (if it's true) that you would like to talk more at a later time.

3 — Evaluate:

During the relationship meeting, do not take notes or record anything. Such actions get in the way of the conversation. As soon as possible after the meeting, however, jot down what this person was interested in, where they had the most energy, and what you would like to talk to them about at a later date. These notes become invaluable for continued building of the relationship.

Break	*Host*	**5 minutes**

Role Play	*Session Leader*	**15 minutes**

The Session Leader will choose a willing member of the group and, in front of all, roleplay a 10-minute relationship meeting. Ask the members to note any questions or observations and at the end of roleplay take 5 minutes to answer question and note any insights.

| **Activity** | *Session Leader* | **20 minutes** |

Pair up members and have them practice relationship meetings, having one partner designated as the questioner for the first 10 minutes and then switching roles for the final 10 minutes.

| **Debrief (plenary)** | *Session Leader* | **10 minutes** |

*How did this exercise feel?

*Did you find out something about your partner that you didn't know before?

*Any surprises? Any difficulties?

| **Plan** | *Session Leader* | **10 minutes** |

(It may be helpful to have a list of the members of the church available for reference. Don't forget newcomers who may not yet be in the directory! As you make assignments put them up on newsprint and keep this for the next session.)

Together, decide who each member will have a relationship meeting with before the next session. Try to do at least two, and if possible up to four. Everyone has different commitments and schedules to contend with, but remember...the relationship meetings themselves take only 30-45 minutes of your time.

RELATIONSHIP MEETING

What it is about	What it is not about
Relationship	Task
Active, long-term listening (asking for a relationship)	Talk
Their Interests	My Interests
Their Energy	My Energy
Making an offer of power/empowerment in their areas of interest	Selling
Probing with respectful boundaries	Prying or chit-chat
Getting to personal reasons for public action	Voyeurism
Being curious	Stereotyping

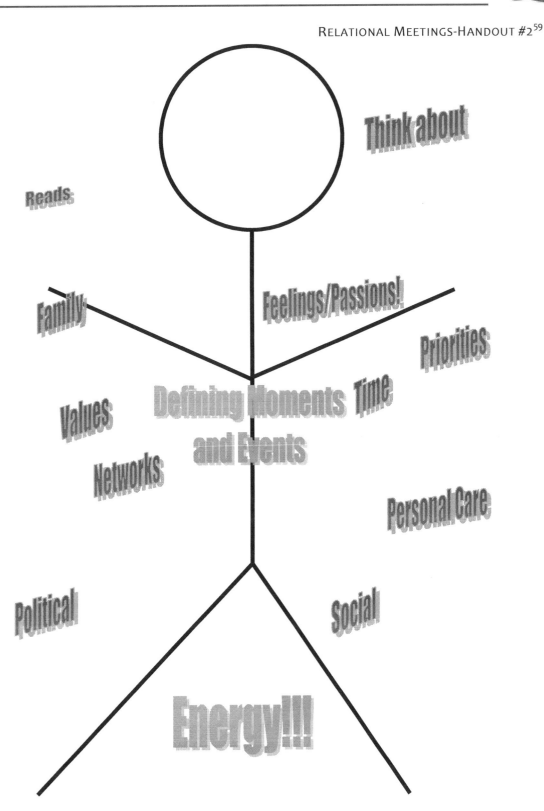

COMMUNITY ORGANIZING:

HOUSE MEETINGS

Description: House meetings are small gatherings of people invited together to discuss areas of interest with the goal of furthering the organizers' understanding of the issues inherent in problems. Organizers are also interested in learning the motivation of the people gathered and seeking potential leaders. While called House Meetings, these gatherings don't have to take place in any particular location. They do, however, need to exude an atmosphere of hospitality and true interest in what the participants have to say.

Format: The gatherings are of 6-10 people, but more than one group can meet at a time (or several groups may meet around the same subject at different times). Each small group will need an organizer to host it, presenting the questions and facilitating the conversation. A recorder, usually another organizer, is also present and taking notes on what is said.

As with Relational meetings, House Meetings have three phases:

1 — Plan:

The first phase is that of planning. In the case of House Meetings, care must be taken to choose a subject which is of interest to the potential participants, usually one which will have several different aspects and viewpoints. Then questions must be carefully crafted to invite the most honest and deep conversation possible. Begin with a question that roots the subject in each individuals experience, such as, "Tell us about a time when you experienced an outreach program that made a difference in your life." Such a personal question can then be followed by a more general question seeking to surface issues around the central "problem". Practice having conversations around the questions with your group of organizers, and then revise them as needed.

Also in the planning stage, an intentional invitation list is created and discussion about how to get participants to the meetings is held. Organizers are assigned to different aspects of this invitational stage.

2 — Act:

Then the organizers act, meaning the House Meeting is convened. A brief statement of the "problem" or area of interest is made, along with the rules of dialogue that will be followed. (I have found the list of principles for conversation found in *Turning to One Another* by Margaret Wheatley succinct and helpful to participants.[60]) The conversation in the small groups should last about 50-60 minutes. The recorder should be noting different issues which come up, as well as who seems to be particularly motivated.

3 — Evaluate:

The evaluation phase is very important and should be done by the organizers directly following the event. Not only will issues which have been raised need to be noted, and potential leaders identified to the whole group, but the level of success of various aspects of the House Meeting should be examined. Did you get the number of participants you planned for, and if not, why not? Were the instructions and questions clear? Were hosts and recorders functioning well? All these aspects of the meeting are evaluated and noted, so the next time around the team builds on their experience and has more confidence.

Indication for Use: House Meetings traditionally follow relational meetings in a process of community organizing. Relational meetings often suggest the topics which should be pursued in House Meetings. However, there is no reason a congregation can't use this exercise on its own, or even before relational meetings are attempted.

House Meetings deepen the capacity for both true communication and deep community in a group of people. They will help sharpen the understanding of what is important to a community and get out the various different issues which might be part of a general problem. They are also venues for participants to discern what kind of leadership style and ability might be present in the group.

Cautions: House Meetings are most successful when they focus on one particular area of interest at a time. One group which attempted to do a House Meeting around the topics of outreach and evangelism at the same time found that, while these topics had much in common, there was not enough unity to keep conversation focused.

Questions also need to be tested beforehand to make sure there is both clear understanding and enough substance to allow participants to dig deep. A practice House Meeting during the planning stage is very helpful.

Directions: On the next pages is an outline for planning House Meetings, as well as a sample agenda of a House Meeting.

OUTLINE FOR PLANNING HOUSE MEETINGS

House Meetings: Plan—Act—Evaluate

PLAN

Goals

1) Relationship Building

2) Finding Leaders (Types handout)

3) Agitate, i.e. find where the energy is centered. Identify themes & problems

Line up players   =   Host and recorder

6-10 people (how will you get them to come?)

Frame   =   How to get to stories you want people to share?

How and where will you meet?

ACT

1) Model behavior by being ready to share first

2) Remember relational meeting techniques

3) Check in with quiet members

4) If more than one small group, gather whole and share highlights

5) Invite to continue relationship

EVALUATE

Meet immediately after with other leaders and recorders to ask:

- How did it feel?
- Turn-out? Did leaders deliver? If not, how in future?
- Time-frame and setting?
- Identification of themes/problems/energy
- Emerging leaders-who and around what?
- What is next step(s) and who will do it (them)?

SAMPLE AGENDA FOR A HOUSE MEETING

CONNECTING WITH OTHERS

Outreach from our Congregation
Sunday 3-5 pm

Schedule:

3pm	Gather, Nametags, Coffee, Introduction of the process
3:15	Divide into small groups for conversation
4:30	Gather groups together for cheese and crackers, and share highlights of small group dialogue
5pm	Thank-you and good day
(5-6:30pm)	Organizing team dinner and debriefing

Small Group Conversation Questions:

I.   Rounds: Please share your name and when you began coming to our church. Why did you decide to join us for this conversation?

II.   Tell us a story about a time when you have either been part of a successful outreach ministry or the recipient of one. What made it successful and how was it important?

III.   How do you feel our congregation might grow in outreach ministries?

GOSPEL-BASED DISCIPLESHIP BIBLE STUDY

Description: The Gospel-Based Discipleship Bible study is a method of inviting people to have a dialogue or conversation about a Bible passage (which really doesn't have to be out of the gospels), instead of a discussion or debate. The goal is for each participant to listen to how God is speaking to them through the reading, and then to share it with the other members of the group. There is no judgment made about the most "correct" interpretations. All viewpoints are equally welcomed and valued.

Format: A Bible passage is chosen (either by the group or by the group leader). It will be read three times, either by one person or by different voices. You may also choose to either have the three readings from the same translation or different translations.

Three questions are asked, one after each reading, so the rhythm is: Ask the question. Read the passage. Ask the question again. Then wait for all who would like to respond to do so. Repeat the sequence with a different question two more times, going deeper into the passage. There should be no pressure for anyone to speak but encouragement (and enough patience with silence) for everyone to offer their insights.

If this exercise is part of a longer meeting or class, the Bible can be left in the center of the group and the passage referred back to at any time. This reminds participants that theirs is a community grounded in God's word, and ties insights about our relationship with God to learning and decision making.

Indications for use: This is a wonderful exercise to level the playing field in vertically hierarchical congregations where members always look to the ordained minister for answers. People new to the concept may feel uncomfortable at first, disclaiming their responses as not being educated or sophisticated. With enough encouragement though, the experience of the exercise itself will prove that God speaks to everyone, no matter what their level of schooling, through the Word. We all, including rectors and pastors, can learn from each other's insights.

Cautions: While there is no situation which would preclude Gospel Based Discipleship bible study, be clear about the goal of sharing insights instead of determining a correct interpretation. Those participants who are used to Bible study discussions may have difficulty refraining from arguing and offering proof that their insights are correct. Indeed, those of us who regularly study the Bible may not be able to hear certain passages without scholarly commentary ringing in our ears. That's ok, as long as we offer those viewpoints as just another way to hear the passage and not the "right" way. If you are leading the study, and dialogue begins to turn into debate, gently remind people of the goal of sharing.

Description: The three questions most often used to direct the Bible study are:

1) What word, idea or sentence stands out for you in this passage?

2) What is God saying to you in this reading?

3) What is God calling you (or your community) to do?

There may be times when you will want to modify or come up with different questions. That's fine, as long as they are open-ended and allow for freedom of insights.

A NIGHT TO REMEMBER

(See also Alban Institute's *Discerning Your Congregation's Future*)[61]

Description: The goal of this 3-4 hour workshop is to help your congregation articulate central values which form the core of its corporate identity. It does this through a guided construction of a church timeline and dialogue about what has been important to members throughout the years.

Format: For this workshop, you will want as many of the congregation's members present as possible, as it is important to include as many memories and viewpoints as possible.

The first half of the exercise is the construction of a timeline. Butcher paper on a long wall makes a good surface to record on. Current events can be posted to help people remember and get oriented to particular time periods (i.e. Pearl Harbor Day, First Moon Walk, etc.). I also find it helpful to have already recorded the various pastors or rectors under their years of service. Working from the present time and moving backwards, the parishioners tell stories of what was important during these years in their church life, and notes are recorded beneath the dates.

The second half of the workshop invites members to reflect on their history by generating "meaning statements", i.e. declaration (either positive or negative) of what has consistently been important to community. Out of this conversation, a sense of identity is articulated.

Indications for use: This workshop can be used as an exercise for exploring the congregation's past and present. Whether it is the initial time your church has investigated the foundation of its personality or a subsequent revisiting of its history and identity, new insights are sure to be gleaned. This workshop is especially helpful if there is not patience for a longer session, such as the Congregational Identity workshop requires, but still a desire to dialogue about the meaning of historical events and memories.

Cautions: If you cannot bring together the majority of the congregation for this effort, be aware that some members may feel left out and marginalized. If possible, leave up the timeline and notes, with the meaning statements, and encourage those who couldn't attend to add stories and comment on the results.

Directions: This workshop is described in-depth in the book from Alban Institute entitled *Discerning Your Congregation's Future* (see pp. 65-75). I have also included below an example agenda, planned around a potluck meal and dessert, as well as my introduction to the workshop.

A Night to Remember

An Example Agenda

5:30-9:30pm

Materials Needed:
1) Timeline with Pastorate/Interims on top line and current events on bottom with lots of room in middle
2) Markers
3) Vestry ready to facilitate small groups
4) Paper and pencils for small groups
5) Easel and paper pad
6) Dots for voting

5:30-6   **Settle and get dinner** (Introductory rounds in table groups: "The reason I started at and stay part of our church is...")

6-6:15   **Explanation of evening* and opening prayer**

6:15-7:30   **Construction of Timeline**
Begin with current year and move backwards. Whole group participates brainstorming most important events that took place during pastorate or interim period — good, bad, happy or sad.

7:30-7:40   ----BREAK (for dessert!)----

7:40-8:35   **Developing Meaning Statements** (generalizations based on observations about history)
A) In table groups: Generate meaning statements (25 min)
B) Facilitator reports to plenary–record + and – lists. (20 min)
C) Whole group votes on priority of meaning statements (10 min)

8:35-9:30   **Closing Meditation**
A) Guided Imagery (10 min) pp. 73-74 of *Discerning Your Congregation's Future*
B) Sharing and praying with partner (15 min)
C) End with Lord's Prayer

EXPLANATION OF THE EVENING

The goal of "A Night to Remember" is to tell our congregation's story. Because every one of you has experienced this story in different ways, it's important to have all of you here to give your view of the ups and downs, the sorrows and joys of life at our church. Like the picture in a stained glass window -- it doesn't make sense until all the colors are in place. We also need the dark lines of the lead in the stained glass window to get the picture... and in our church story we have to hear the bad, the difficult and the sorrowful as well as the high points and joy, to get the whole picture of who we are in this congregation.

Telling the complete, deep story of our past in this congregation will both help us understand the present and give us guidelines to what we want to build on and what we want to heal in the future. So, tonight we will do the following:

1) First of all, we will together construct a timeline of what has happened at our church, then

2) Consider what is meaningful about that history that we want to work on in the future, and

3) Finally, end in prayer that will invite God to work with us/through us as we move into that future.

THE CONGREGATIONAL IDENTITY WORKSHOP

Description: This workshop is designed to enable members to articulate their congregation's personality. In the process, they will learn about other church styles which challenge or affirm their own identity, providing insight into future development. This workshop is not based on scientific measurements or calculations. Instead, it is a process intended to help a group of people paint a verbal portrait of their church community.

Format: While originally designed for a vestry or governing board, this workshop is richest if the whole congregation can participate. It will take either one 6-7 hour day or two 3 hour segments scheduled no more than a week apart.

The first half of the workshop creates a focused timeline of the congregation's historical and present life, using questions which elicit stories of ministry, mission, theology, stewardship and evangelism. It also invites reflection on the congregation's weaknesses. This exercise is structured to encourage the inclusion of each participant's voice and viewpoint.

The second half of the workshop utilizes typology created by Carl Dudley and Sally Johnson in their study of mainline denominations, "Energizing the Congregation"[62] . Participants are given background descriptions of the five types of church personalities that emerged in this study, and led through an exercise to investigate what attributes might make up their communal identity. A conversation about both the process and the findings is then encouraged to provide a solid foundation for the exploration of edges of growth and development.

Indication for Use: This is a workshop to use when exploring the congregation's past and present identity. Although lengthy, it will help participants gain a more balanced view of who their congregation truly is, and provide common language for continued dialogue about development.

Cautions: If you decide to split this workshop into two sections, be aware that it is very disruptive to have members join the second session who have not been to the first. People who cannot be present for the workshop can be folded in later, by explaining the "Congregational Pie Chart" which will be created and by reviewing the timeline.

This workshop does take some set-up time. Be sure that leaders read through the directions and have on hand the needed tools, including the pie chart blown up to poster size.

It is assumed that the leader of the workshop will have the skill set of a small group facilitator. Either an in-house leader or someone from the wider community could take this role. It is also very helpful if the leader of a Congregational Identity Workshop is able to easily think in metaphorical terms.

Directions: Below is an explanation of how to do the Congregational Identity Workshop. For the background on its development, see my doctoral thesis, "Passport to the Future"[63].

CONGREGATIONAL IDENTITY WORKSHOP EXAMPLE

(Two fictional parishes are used as examples in the commentary below. St. Swithin's is a small congregation of about 25 regularly attending members which shares a pastor with another small church. St. Dymphna's is a mid-sized parish of around 150-200 attending on Sundays and one full time pastor.)

Participants:
> A general invitation to all the members of the congregation is recommended. Special care should be taken to stress the importance of leaders, such as governing board members, worship leaders, teachers etc. to be present. It's also especially important to extend personal invitations to new members who may not feel they have been around long enough to have much to add, or members on the periphery. Often, their viewpoints will illuminate values of the church which the mainstream is overlooking. Don't forget young adults and youth.

Goals of the workshop:
> 1) Create an environment for the raising up of stories and memories which articulate shared themes and symbols.
> 2) Distill the information gathered from stories into a user-friendly presentation which a congregation can revisit as new people join, integrating their perceptions and celebrating their evolving identity.
> 3) Help church members articulate their personality in such a way that they can use it as a positive foundation for development, keeping their identity intact as they grow.

Workshop Materials:
> - A comfortable room with tables to seat small groups (for the time line exercise), which allows the whole group to hear and converse
> - A timeline of paper on the wall with years marked off in decades
> - Large easel and pad of paper
> - Markers of different colors
> - Individual "pie charts" for each participant (plus some extra)
> - A large "pie chart" for the easel
> - Enough highlighters to go around and a set with different colors (8 if possible) for the leader
> - Tape or thumbtack

INTRODUCTION OF WORKSHOP (10-15 minutes)
Stress the purpose of the workshop as the creation of a picture or metaphor of the congregation's personality. Explain the difference between sign and symbol/metaphor. Emphasize that this workshop does not deal with hard facts but shares experiences and perceptions. Encourage participants to share openly, as every opinion, experience and perception is valid and valuable.

Commentary:
The introduction of the workshop is crucial to its success, although it will take only 10-15 minutes. If people are halfway through the process and discover it is not producing the kind of information they expected, no amount of back pedaling will be able to pull everyone together and on track. After people have arrived and an opening prayer has been said, the leader needs to clearly state the goal of the workshop: "What we are here to do today is to paint a picture, to create a metaphor, of this congregation's personality." It may be necessary at this point to explain the difference between a sign and a symbol/metaphor. I often draw a stop sign on the easel and ask the group what it means. Since they all will say "stop" in one way or another, I can point out that signs have one clear meaning. Then I draw a cross and ask what that means. The group will inevitably come up with many answers, from Christ to crucifixion to salvation. Of course, they are all correct which allows for the leader to point out that a metaphor is like the symbol of the cross. It has layers of meaning and there are various ways to view it. It's like the difference between a Polaroid snapshot and a portrait painted by a great artist. The work done together in the workshop will provide a metaphor, i.e. an in-depth portrait of the congregation's identity.

When you are sure the group understands the goal, there are two other points to make. First of all, this workshop does not provide a "scientific" or hard data assessment of the church. Instead it is a way of sharing experiences and perceptions in a process which will enable a corporate vision of the congregation to emerge. It may seem redundant to say this after spelling out the goal, but people who are right brain dominant and looking for the "facts" will need to have this expectation raised and dismissed. Secondly, because this process depends on people sharing, take some time to reassure participants that every opinion, experience and perception is valid and valuable. Encourage them to be as open and authentic as possible.

THE TIME-LINE (2-3 HOURS)

Place placards on the tables available with a decade of years on it (for example 1960s, 1970s, 1980s etc.). Ask members to sit at the decade table which includes the year they joined the congregation. If one table has more than twelve participants, ask them to divide themselves up into five year increments. Choose a scribe for each group.

A. At each table ask the members to give answer to the following questions about the years that they joined: (Have the scribe record everyone's answers, even if in disagreement.)

1. How did the church fit into the community?
2. What kind of ministry were you all doing and who was leading?
3. Who were you working with in ministry?
4. How did the priest view God? Did the majority of laity agree?
5. What social ministries were you engaged in?
6. How did you work at stewardship?
7. How did you bring others into the church?
8. What was the main weakness of the church?

B. When each table has had enough time, call the group back together and beginning with the oldest group, record their answers under the years they represent.

C. Move on to ask the same questions of the next group in chronological order. After they have had a chance to respond, let the group before them give input as to how they perceived the church at this time. Note any differences. As you move forward on the timeline, every person should have a chance to be the main "definer" of the year they joined, but also have a voice in any year they were present.

D. In plenary, answer the eight questions and note responses for the present year.

Commentary:

In each small group, the members will be asked to answer eight questions, pertaining solely to the time when they first joined the church. Write the focus questions on the easel for the group to refer to as you progress. Each participant may have very different answers to these questions, even in the same decade (even in the same year!) and an effort must be made to acknowledge that such differences are welcomed and expected. The scribe at each table should faithfully record the gist of all answers. Take the group through one question at a time, even though some groups will finish faster than others.

When all the small groups have had a chance to answer the questions for their decades, begin with the earliest decade group and note their responses on the newsprint below their years. As you move on to the next group, return to the first respondents after recording their answers, to see if a different or additional observation was made. As you progress through the years, each group will have a chance to be in the spotlight sharing their perceptions, but the other members who were present in that year will also have valuable insights to be noted. When you come to the current year, everyone gets equal time as they voice their current experience of the church.

The focus questions are designed to stimulate group discussion around the central issues addressed in each of the universal church images developed by Dudley and Johnson in their book, "Energizing the Congregation." As the workshop members answer the focus questions, the stories and explanations offered will lift up symbols and themes common to the community. The questions are as follows:

1. **How did (does) the church fit into the community?**
    This question seeks to uncover the context of the church in its neighborhood, as the members saw it. Many members of the workshop, as evidenced at both St. Dymphna's and St. Swithin's, may have trouble articulating how other people in the community saw the church, but they can describe their first impressions of finding the church, worshiping and getting to know people. As with all the focus questions, the leader may rephrase this question to help get people started, as long as the intent of the question is clear. With our fictional parishes, if members responded that they had no idea how the church fit into the community, the facilitator urged them to remember and recount how and why they began attending and how their first experiences felt to them.

2. **What kind of ministry were (are) you doing and who was (is) leading?**
    This question seeks information about the focus of mission in the church and about activities in which the members were invested. It turned out, however, that in the test workshops as this process was being developed, the participants uniformly answered this question with in-house activities, and so a more specific question about outreach ministries was added (see question 5). St. Swithin's members, though, had a more extensive understanding of ministry which

included outreach to the community. They wanted to share those ministries under this question, so the leader had to be explicit about wanting to hear what ministries occurred at the church on Sundays and week nights, while reassuring the speakers that the outreach efforts would be recorded under a different question. As you can see, flexibility is important when directing this portion of the workshop. Remember, how the information is gained is not as important as important as noting it on the time-line. People will generally sort it out well for themselves later.

3.   **Who were you working with in ministry?**
Here, the leader is asking the members to remember other churches or social organizations with whom their parish has worked in partnership. A regional or national organization may be mentioned, as well.

4.   **How did the priest or pastor view God? Did the majority of the laity agree?**
This is the hardest question for members of the group to really grasp or discuss. The facilitator may ask the participants to try to remember what kind of sermons the pastor presented or how he or she related to the members in the church. Usually this elicits stories of how the person remembers relating to the clergy. To ask if the majority of laity agreed with the theology of the pastor may bring up memories of church conflicts and disagreements. Again, don't worry too much about sorting this out. Just make notes to remind everyone of the issues raised.

Another point to consider when this question is raised for the current year, or any year in which the pastor in charge is present, is how honest people feel they can be in the pastor's presence. When the group reaches the point when this becomes an issue, stop and discuss how everyone feels about it before forging ahead. For the pastors of both St. Swithin's and St. Dymphna's, this exercise turned out to be very affirming of their ministries, and raised no conflicts of which they were unaware. In fact, the hardest part for both of them was trying to express their view of God... in less time than it takes to preach a sermon!

4.   What social ministries were (are) you engaged in?
Now is the time to probe for outreach ministries, i.e. any organized work for the benefit of groups outside the church. Many congregations open their doors to house groups they don't necessarily work with, and this is the place to note those relationships, also.

6.   How did (do) you work at stewardship?
No one misunderstands this question. Usually the stories of fundraising around operating budgets and building campaigns are very vivid. At St. Dymphna's, the stewardship committee had been working on promoting a understanding of stewardship that included more than just financial resources, and those efforts were noted under this question, too.

7.   How did (do) you bring others into church?
Many people are not aware of any evangelism efforts, especially in their early years in the congregation. The leader may direct members to think about how they themselves found out about the church and made the decision to start attending. Then, members may also remember how people who became friends happened to join. Note here that some denominations have a real prejudice against the word "evangelism", while others embrace the concept.

8.   What was (is) the main weakness of the church?
At St. Swithin's, where the early years of the church were in great contrast with its present condition, there was some difficulty in articulating anything negative about its "golden era". As the facilitator progressed through the time-line, however, the older members began to remember some flaws in those years and it was simple to go back and note them. They had just needed some time to get their rose colored glasses off.

The groups at St. Dymphna's were in total agreement about what the weaknesses of the congregation were in all the years they explored, except the current date where they disagreed vehemently. The leader simply noted each position very carefully on the newsprint.

A few members may object to focusing on a negative. If so, remind them of two things: First, we have explored seven very positive aspects of the church in each of the other questions. Second, often a weakness is a two-edged sword indicating a hidden strength. If we acknowledge it, we may be able to turn it to our advantage.

THE PIE CHART (2-3 HOURS) (TEMPLATE PROVIDED BELOW)

A.   Put the large pie chart up on the tripod so everyone can see it. Explain Dudley and Johnson's five church types (see below), using the pie chart to point out the various differences. Stress that none of these types is better than the other and that all 40 churches used to develop these templates had vital and valid ministries. Also stress that this is not an exact science with right and wrong answers, but rather the best guess of people who have lived in these communities. We are painting a picture with broad strokes… not taking photographs for evidence!

B.   Discuss with the group which "type" they think might have fit their church in its early days. Note their responses on the time-line.

C.   Hand out the individual pie charts and a highlighter to each member of the workshop. Have each person turn now to their own pie chart and instruct them to work alone. Tell them to mark their pie charts where they think their congregation currently fits in each of the eight categories. They may divide their answers between types but must limit their responses to one per question. Again, remind them that there are no right or wrong answers… simply perceptions.

D.   When all have completed the above, bring the group back together and, starting with question # 1, tally up the responses on the big pie chart. As you go, note how many responses you have in each category and in each type on the chart. Then color in approximately how many responses you have in each pie slice, using a different color for each question. The goal is to end up with a visual chart of where their answers fall. Be sure to allow for discussion of why people answered the way they did, especially encouraging those in the minority to voice their feelings and insights. Do not allow judgments on any member's perceptions. All opinions are valid and valuable.

E.   Take a few minutes to reflect silently on the pattern of identity which has emerged on the big chart. Then initiate discussion on what the members have learned. You may want to use the questions from "Questions for Wrapping up the C.I. Workshop".

F.   Reflect on the overall experience of the workshop. Was it helpful? What did you like best/least? What would you change?

Commentary:

After the focused time-line has been completed, you are ready to go on to the last portion of the workshop. Allow two to three hours for this portion. It goes quickly at first, but people will need time at the end for unhurried reflection and discussion. Now is the time to put up the large copy of the pie-chart, or project it on the wall. The first step is to explain the nature of the church types. [64]

In their study of 40 congregations, Dudley and Johnson discovered that churches revealed similar sets of images. Admittedly, they were looking for these images within the context of the Christian faith.

 Out of their research, Dudley and Johnson felt that they could group the images which surfaced into five universal types, within which all 40 churches could be categorized. These types are: Pillar Church, Pilgrim Church, Survivor Church, Prophet Church and Servant Church.

As facilitator you should point out, when these types are introduced, that the eight questions used for the focused time-line exercise were developed to correspond with the areas which Dudley and Johnson used to develop these universal images. For your convenience, a description of each type and how members of such a church would ideally respond to each question is provided below. Members of groups at both St. Swithin's and St. Dymphna's had no problem grasping this concept, even though their leaders presented this material in a very informal and cursory way:

Both the **Pillar** and the **Pilgrim** church types have their identity rooted in a sense of responsibility, with the Pillar type firmly anchored in the geographic area and the Pilgrim type focusing on a group of people. "The Pillar church cares about the place, the whole community, for which it feels accountable to God. The Pilgrim church provides the focus of faith and culture for a particular people."

The typical member of the **Pillar** church would:
   1)   See the congregation as the cornerstone church of their area, front and center in the community, the most prominent parish in town.
   2)   Ministry would focus on worship and education, with the goal being to equip people to help themselves.

3) Partners in ministry would include other churches (with which this church works best, often organizing ecumenical associations) and they also don't hesitate to seek professional expertise.
4) Theologically, this pastor and congregation run from liberal to moderate.
5) They tend to be conservative on social issues.
6) The most organized of the church types in stewardship, they have detailed budgets supported by annual pledges and a few fundraisers.
7) In contrast, they don't have a highly organized evangelical effort, but depend on strong community associations to bring people into the congregation.
8) The greatest weakness of this kind of church is its tendency to develop a "fortress mentality" which draws a very clear boundary between who is in and who is out.

The **Pilgrim** church expresses its responsible personality in a much different way. The answers its typical member would give to the eight questions are as follows:

1) While not the most prominent church in the community, the pilgrim church is known as one which identifies with a certain culture or group. Often this is a minority group. An example I often use is the Korean Baptist Church, but you will probably know of others in your area. It may not be a cultural or social group which this congregation is focused on, however. Little St. Swithin's found that a great deal of its identity meshed with this type, because its denomination was rare in their part of the country.
2) It is not surprising that a congregation which identifies with a particular minority group would then have a ministry emphasis on reaching out and adopting others. They tend to be especially active with caring for children and families.
3) The pilgrims work best with similar cultural or theological groups.
4) Their theology is moderate-very mainstream for whatever their denomination happens to be.
5) This is the most liberal of churches when it comes to social issues.
6) The Pilgrim church's stewardship efforts may not be highly organized, but they always appeal to the loyalty of their members for support. You might suggest that this is like a family, which doesn't always take time to print out a budget but expects everyone to pitch in to pay the bills.
7) Pilgrim churches bring people into the fold through events like weddings and funerals, as well as other associations with family

members. It grows when outsiders are exposed to the warmth of the community life and want to be part of the family. 8) Much like the Pillar church, though, the greatest weakness of this type is its tendency to separate from the surrounding community and become ingrown.

Two other types of churches, the **Survivor** and the **Prophet**, lift up the major theme of dealing with crises in their lives, although in very different ways.

"Survivor churches are reactive, always responding to crises that come upon them, barely able to keep up. Prophet churches are proactive, converting particular situations into campaigns to challenge and transform some larger evil in the world." [65]

The **Survivor** church member would answer the eight questions in the following manner.

1) These congregations are often located in declining neighborhoods. The parish itself may be teetering on the edge of extinction.

2) The Survivor church understands ministering to people in crisis better than any other church type, and these crisis ministries, such as food and clothing banks, counseling services and shelters, come most naturally to them.

3) Because existence seems so tenuous for this congregation, they will accept help that is offered, like donations of food or money to keep services going, but tend to be the least open of the church types to any partnerships. This may be because they are afraid other churches would simply overwhelm them, or that they don't have enough to reciprocate in the relationship.

4) Pastors and members of the Survivor church tend to be evangelical to moderate in their theology.

5) Dealing, as they do, with the very disadvantaged of society, these people are most often liberal on social issues.

6) Very little of the Survivor church's energy goes into formal fundraising. They depend instead on gifts and mission funding to make ends meet.

7) The Survivor church grows as people with personal difficulties find a home there, and become strong enough to commit to a community.

8) The greatest weakness the Survivor church displays is a feeling of being overwhelmed by the immensity of the problems in the world and its own limited resources. Such feelings may lead members to retreat into themselves or, in the worst case scenario, to give up all together.

The proactive **Prophet** church members would respond to the eight focus question in a much different way, although they share the Survivor church's concern with the state of the world.

1) This congregation would have a higher profile in their community. While not as generally prominent as the Pillar type, this church may be on the evening news more and is known as the congregation on the leading edge of activism.

2) Unlike the Survivor church which deals with the crises close to home, the Prophet church takes on global, world-changing opportunities. They may organize protests over capital punishment or bring in refugees from South America.

3) This church type works best with social agencies. Other churches usually move too slowly for its sense of urgency.

4) The most diverse in its theology, the pastor and people of the Prophet church may be evangelical, moderate or liberal in their theology.

5) Like the Survivor and the Pilgrim types, this congregation tends to be liberal socially.

6) More than any other type, the Prophet church is serious about sacrificial giving, preaches about tithing and then commits a portion of its own budget to ministries and causes outside of the congregation.

7) People are attracted to this congregation through the projects it has championed. They join as they are willing to work towards the ministry goals which they see being lived out in the world.

8) The weakness of a Prophet church is really two fold. On the one hand, the members can become so involved in their causes that, in the heat of the battle, they lose sight of why they are fighting. They also may be plagued with leadership problems, either too dependent on a charismatic leader or immobilized by their need for consensus.

The final type, the **Servant** church, has a dominant story of simply caring for people. "Servants see individuals in need and reach out to help them in supportive and pastoral ministries. They live their faith in simple service."[66] Dudley and Johnson found the Servant type to be the most prevalent among the churches they studied.

This kind of congregation would respond to the focus questions in the following manner:

1) While this is not the most prominent church in town, it is an established and respected member of the neighborhood.

2) The Servant congregation prefers simple practical care in response to individuals. Their women's groups may organize to bring casseroles to

members' families when illness strikes. Their men's group may go around the neighborhood fixing up houses for senior citizens they know. There's not a lot of fanfare or recognition of these ministries. They are low key, quiet and done simply because someone in the congregation recognizes a need which can be addressed.

3) True to their low key profile, the Servant church works best in its own neighborhood with other near-by churches.

4) The pastor and members of the Servant church have a moderate, mainline theology.

5) These members are the most conservative on social issues.

6) The Servant church is not big on organized fundraising. The congregation finds that money is always tight, but somehow they always manage to make ends meet.

7) The Servant type church attracts people who see their Christianity calling them to practical everyday ministries and who want to work. Another unique characteristic of this church is that it is the only type which focuses evangelism efforts on "backsliders", i.e. members who have, for one reason or another, quit coming to church.

8) The major downside of the Servant church, however, is that because of its non-judgmental and gentle style of neighborhood caring, the members can create dependency in the people they help.

Once you have explained the characteristics of each of the five church types, go back to the focused time-line you created and discuss with the group which "type" their church might have been in the earliest days. Note their responses on the time-line. Then move about half-way down the line and repeat this for the middle years.

At the workshops with St. Dymphna's and St. Swithin's, members found this exercise fairly easy to do. St. Dymphna members understood that in its early days the congregation was a strong Prophet Type church. Twenty to thirty years into its life, however, the parish lost this focus and took on many of the attributes of a Survivor church, even though Prophet characteristics still remained. Great energy was created around the recognition of this major shift in identity, with some expression that it was a relief to have this spelled out.

At St. Swithin's, consensus was harder to come by. They were pretty evenly split between placing its early years in the Pillar category or the Pilgrim category. The leader simply put both types up as equal definitions. As they moved onto the middle years however this congregation, like St. Dymphna's, experienced a real change in identity. Their personality shift seemed to veer towards Survivor and Servant characteristics. The fact that the small town within which St. Swithin's resides was undergoing a major identity change at the time was also raised up and discussed.

After looking at the two periods in history on the time-line (or more if the history of the church seems to warrant it), turn to the present. Hand out the individual blank pie charts and a highlighter to each member of the workshop. Explain that though Dudley and Johnson fit each of the forty churches they interviewed into one of these "types", most church members will see parts of their congregation in more than just one image. The pie charts before them will help paint a portrait which will show their church's personality in a more in-depth and accurate way.

Ask each participant to work by themselves and, considering their congregation as it is right now, highlight one section of the of the "pie" in response to each of the eight focus questions. They may want to refer to the time-line notes that were made earlier. Stress that, while they may color any section under any church type, they need to limit their responses to one per question. They should also be reminded to mark an answer to question eight, found up in the corners.

There was some concern at St. Swithin's, because questions #4 and #5 have answers that are the same under different church types. The leader reminded the participants that this was not hard fact gathering, but a time for gut responses. An answer is neither wrong nor right, and the participants should make a choice out of their intuition about where their congregation fits best. It also helped to assure the members that their responses would be discussed and, if they should want to change them later, they could.

At St. Swithin's and St. Dymphna's this exercise of highlighting areas of the pie chart went fairly quickly (10-15 minutes), even with some grousing going on. Note here, though, that some people may have trouble completing their chart. At St. Swithin's, an elderly woman had misunderstood the instructions and was too embarrassed to ask for help. In the St. Dymphna group, one middle-aged man dug in his heels and refused to make choices that didn't seem factual to him. The leader in both of these cases wisely didn't push for compliance. Instead, these people were invited to join in the next exercise of comparing the individual charts and simply add their opinions with the rest of the group. In this way, they found a venue to share their experiences that was more comfortable for them. The important thing is to include all the participants as fully as possible.

After everyone has completed their pie chart, the whole group can be brought back together for the next portion of the workshop which involves comparing these charts and discussing their answers.

Starting with question #1, tally up their responses on the big "pie chart". As you go, color in with your highlighter approximately how many members choose each answer. (For example: If everyone chose #1 under the Pillar Church type, you would color in the whole #1 pie slice under Pillar. If only half choose it, you would shade in only half the slice and color appropriate sections of #1 under other types.)

Use a different color for each question, if you have that many highlighters. The goal is to end up with a visual chart of where the members' answers fall. Be sure to allow for discussion of why people answered the way they did, especially encouraging those in the minority to voice their feelings and insights. Do not allow judgments on any member's perceptions. All opinions are valid and valuable.

The creation of a pattern from the comparison of the individual charts was illuminating to the members in the groups from St. Swithin's and St. Dymphna's. The discussion around each question and how participants had come to their conclusions lifted up insights and revelations for all. As they counted up the totals at St. Swithin's (which instead of doing one big workshop had done three smaller ones), two groups came out with a majority of their answers in the Servant category, and a strong secondary emphasis in the Survivor type. The third workshop had the emphasis flipped around, with the majority of responses indicating a Survivor church and the second most popular being the Servant type. Each group noticed, however, that all five church types were represented in their little congregation...which gave them reason to wonder if part of the strength of their church was its ability to include many different expressions of faith.

Later, when members of all the workshops came together and compared their group charts, the people in the third group were able to convey to the others a sense that they treasured the Survivor part of their identity. While participants of the other groups had a tendency to see this as something to grow out of, these members found in the Survivor type a compelling sense of ministry and affirmed its importance to the community as a whole. All group members at St. Swithin's, while hoping for easier financial times for their little congregation, left the week-end with a renewed sense of the power of their Christian witness and a positive feeling about their identity.

At St. Dymphna's, the workshop created an identity pattern in which the Prophet type was most prominent. Members of the governing board, though, had given the Pilgrim type secondary prominence, while other committee leaders saw Servant characteristics as almost equal in strength to the Prophet emphasis. Participants recognized that having both Prophet and Servant characteristics represented a stress in their community which many had felt, but had not been able to describe. Now they saw two sub-groups of their church which had very different styles of relating and doing ministry. The whole group realized that the Servant type was not represented at all in the place where decisions were made, and that the board had been unaware of this tension. As the discussion continued, the positive aspects of being home to divergent expressions of faith were raised and plans initiated for exploring more closely this aspect of their personality while continuing to cherish their strong Prophet identity.

Below are suggested discussion questions to lead participants, both after they have completed a workshop and when two or more groups come together to compare identity charts. These questions are not meant to define the conversation, but are offered simply as a way to begin.

Remember, what shows up on the charts is not as important as the experience of the process. At most, these visual metaphors of the congregation's identity give members a way to reflect on the journey of self-discovery they have just taken and articulate those findings with others.

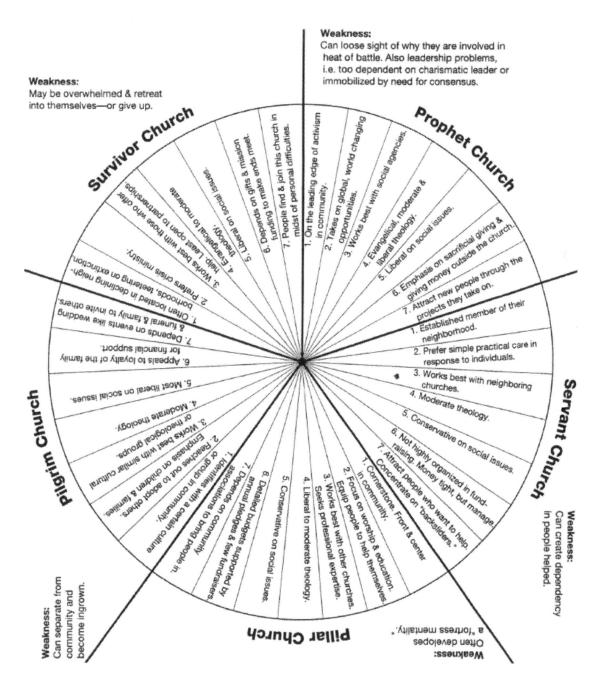

Weakness:
Can loose sight of why they are involved in heat of battle. Also leadership problems, i.e. too dependent on charismatic leader or immobilized by need for consensus.

Weakness:
May be overwhelmed & retreat into themselves—or give up.

Weakness:
Can separate from community and become ingrown.

Weakness:
Can create dependency in people helped.

Weakness:
Often develops a "fortress mentality."

Survivor Church
1. Often located in declining neighborhoods, teetering on extinction.
2. Works best with those who offer help. Least open to partnerships.
3. Evangelical to moderate theology.
4. Liberal on social issues.
5. Depends on gifts & mission funding to make ends meet.
6. People find & join this church in midst of personal difficulties.

Prophet Church
1. On the leading edge of activism in community.
2. Takes on global, world changing opportunities.
3. Works best with social agencies.
4. Evangelical, moderate & liberal theology.
5. Liberal on social issues.
6. Emphasis on sacrificial giving & giving money outside the church.
7. Attract new people through the projects they take on.

Servant Church
1. Established member of their neighborhood.
2. Prefer simple practical care in response to individuals.
3. Works best with neighboring churches.
4. Moderate theology.
5. Conservative on social issues.
6. Not highly organized in fund-raising. Money tight, but manage.
7. Attract people who want to help.

Pillar Church
1. Cornerstone. Front & center in community.
2. Focus on worship & education. Equip people to help themselves.
3. Works best with other churches. Seeks professional expertise.
4. Liberal to moderate theology.
5. Conservative on social issues.
6. Detailed budgets & annual pledges & few fundraisers.
7. Attract people who want to "backsliders." Concentrate on

Pilgrim Church
1. Identifies with a certain culture or group in community.
2. Reaches out to adopt others.
3. Emphasis on children & families or theological groups.
4. Moderate theology.
5. Most liberal on social issues.
6. Appeals to loyalty of the family for financial support.
7. Depends on events like wedding & funeral & family to invite others.
7. Depends on community associations to bring people in.

QUESTIONS FOR WRAPPING-UP THE CONGREGATIONAL IDENTITY WORKSHOP

1.   *What surprises you about the pattern we have just created?*

2.   *Does the personality the chart describes ring true to your experience of the church?*

3.   *Are you happy with the identity shown here or would you like it to change?*

4.   *Does this raise any ideas about where you should be going in the future?*

5.   *What issues does this raise that it would be helpful to explore later?*

ROOTED IN GOD: MOVING FROM MAINTENANCE TO MISSION

Description: The goal of *Rooted in God* is congregational formation. It leads a core group of church members through a process of experiential learning which has them in dialogue with each other and the historical church around the question: "Who is God calling us to be?" The course concludes with a workshop for the whole congregation, inviting them to write a rule of life for the church.

Format: Participants meet twice a month for a period of 5-6 months. Portions of three books are assigned and studied, but the core of the work is experiential. Each session includes Bible study, reflection on the readings, an exercise and deep conversation.

It is expected that the participants will include the wider membership of the congregation in the process by informing them of their work and including them in dialogue around the key issues. This is done either by a world café exercise or more informal conversation.

The last exercise of the program is a workshop led by course members for the whole congregation. In this seminar, the highlights of what they have learned are shared. Then all participants work together to craft a rule of life for the congregation, which can guide them in their future development.

Indications for Use: Any congregation, large or small, can use the *Rooted in God* program to help them discover and articulate who God is calling them to be. It is most effective when the leadership is invested and at least 10 percent of the membership is participating in the core program.

Cautions: If a small group without central leadership makes up the membership of the course, there is a danger that their work will not be taken seriously or integrated into the larger identity of the congregation.

It is important to introduce this program as formation and not education. Participants are given no definitive answers but are guided in discovering their own communal relationship with God.

Directions: *Rooted in God* is an online publication, which can be purchased (and then copied for the use of any number of participants) at www.LeaderResources.org. I have provided an example of a newsletter or flyer which may be helpful in advertising the program below.

(Ad for Newsletter)

ROOTED IN GOD: MOVING FROM MAINTENANCE TO MISSION

Rooted in God is a both a program and a process which will help the congregation determine our congregation's unique calling in God's work. Participants will be led through an exploration of what it means to be the Church, and guided on a journey to discern what God is particularly calling their community to become and do.

The program looks at some of the different ways Christian communities have been structured and grown throughout history to help members ask "How can we be the best Christian community possible?" rather than "How can we just get by?" Taking into consideration both the need to nourish and maintain the existing congregation, while also seriously considering Gospel call to share God's love (Missional Theology), members are encouraged to envision a new future for their congregation. Because a church is her people, much of this conversation takes place in the process of individual formation, i.e. exploring who God is calling us to be as the individuals who make up God's family and who do the ministry of the parish. During the program the following objectives are pursued:

> ➢ Introduction of members to the concept of paradigm change in the Church as the movement of the Holy Spirit which continues to work in our midst.
> ➢ Exploration of "power" and "relationship" as it is lived out in our covenant with God.
> ➢ Exploration of the Benedictine understanding of "obedience" and how we might hear and understand God's will in our lives and our community.
> ➢ Exploration of the Benedictine concept of "stability" and assessing the foundation of our present individual faith and the congregation.
> ➢ Exploration of the Benedictine ideal of "transformation" and looking forward to new life in God's Holy Spirit.
> ➢ Writing a "Congregational Rule of Life" which will serve to guide the parish in fully living into our covenant, i.e. our communal life with God, and set the stage for goals long into the future.

While some outside reading is required, the process of *Rooted in God* is mostly experiential and geared toward discussion and interactive learning. Participants come together twice a month for two hours, share leadership responsibilities and creatively engage the material together. Throughout the months when the participants are meeting, the whole congregation will be informed of and invited to grapple with the foundational questions which are being asked. The ending "Rule of Life" workshop will be open to all members of the congregation, with the participants of *Rooted* forming the core group of presenters and discussion leaders.

APPRECIATIVE INQUIRY

Description: Appreciative Inquiry is a process created as a community and business development tool outside the Church which has been molded by several practitioners to serve congregational work. Its defining feature is the use of positive questions to elicit stories revealing the strengths of the community, which can then be built upon. It is a helpful tool in revealing God's unique call to each congregation, and therefore can be used in communal formation.

Format: A team of people is brought together to define the central developmental issues. They then craft questions which will bring out individual's stories about positive experiences around that issue. Sometimes these stories are gathered by individual interviews and other times in a group setting.

Out of the stories, various common themes are distilled. The core team then uses these themes of strength to formulate "provocative propositions", i.e. statements of a positive future for the community in these areas. Setting goals to fulfill these statements is the final piece of the process.

Indications for use: I have found Appreciative Inquiry especially helpful in two instances: 1) When a congregation is depressed and having trouble facing the future and 2) when there is no cohesive leadership at the center of the congregation. Often, these two issues exist together. Appreciative Inquiry is a wonderful method for reminding people of what they value about their congregation and reviving hope in the future. It also empowers emerging leaders by providing a positive experience of gathering the community together.

Cautions: This is a process which is well defined until it gets to setting goals. Especially if you are working with a team of inexperienced leaders and trying to follow a more egalitarian way of distributing power and responsibility, you will need to supplement this process with conversation about how to follow through and support the membership in the goals and actions decided upon.

Directions: I have reproduced a flow chart I put together to explain this process, which is an overview of its components. I would recommend that you also read one of the many books currently available on the subject. *The Thin Book of Appreciative Inquiry*[67] gives a quick summary of the process. *Appreciative Inquiry: A Positive Revolution in Change*[68] goes more deeply into the theory. For larger groups, *The Appreciative Inquiry Summit*[69] would be helpful.

APPRECIATIVE INQUIRY FLOW CHART

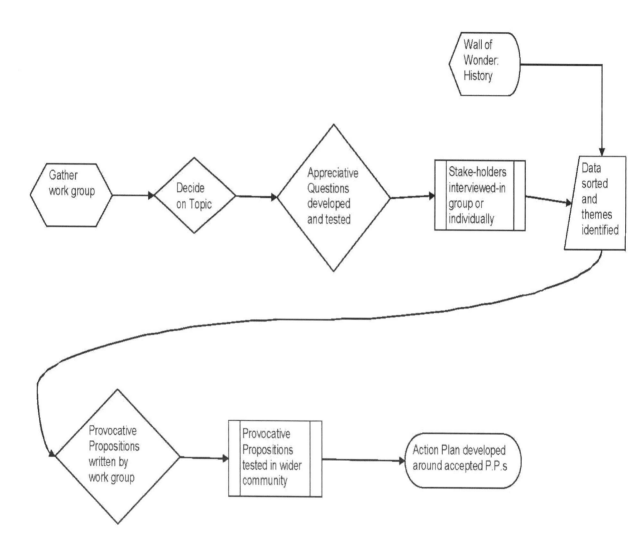

LifeCycles

Description: LifeCycles is a congregational formation process developed specifically to empower churches living into Mutual Ministry. It currently has four cycles of sessions available, each one containing six units with six sessions. The sessions include Bible study, church history, liturgy and spirituality and, most importantly, reflection on the participants' lives both within the congregation and in the world.

Format: LifeCycles is designed to be engaged by a small group of church members. Each session runs 1½-2 hours. Groups often meet around a meal on a regular evening, but other venues are possible. LifeCycles is extremely flexible, allowing participants to move at their own speed and on a schedule which works for their group. Membership for LifeCycles can be purchased by individual churches or by a judicatory (like a diocese or presbytery – which then gives all its congregations access to the material). Materials are electronic downloads with 24/7 access.

While the LifeCycles sessions can be led by any participant, there is training available for mentors and guides are available to get a group started. This is especially helpful when a congregation has not experienced a formation program before.

Indications for Use: LifeCycles is an excellent process for the ongoing formation of a Mutual Ministry congregation. It can create an encouraging foundation for all the other work which is needed to nurture the development of a congregation in this more democratic culture.

Cautions: It can be very difficult for churches which have been used to a didactic method of learning to embrace a formation program in which the central feature is dialogue between all participants. Sometimes it helps to ramp up to the LifeCycles program by engaging in Rooted in God or Wade in the Water, both programs which explore fundamentals of Mutual Ministry. The good news is that both of these programs are included with a LifeCycles membership.

Directions: More LifeCycles information can be found at www.LeaderResources.org. Also, see the Unit 1 Overview on the following page.

LifeCycles: Cycle I—Forming
Community Through Story
Christian Transformation in Community

UNITS ⇒ Sessions ⇓	UNIT 1 Encountering Our Story	UNIT 2 Gathered by the Spirit	UNIT 3 Sent Forth by the Spirit	UNIT 4 Washed & Renewed	UNIT 5 Fed with Thanksgiving	UNIT 6 Celebrate & Serve the Reign of God
Session #1 Experience	Telling Our Stories	Places where We Gather in Our Lives	Our Own Experiences of Being Sent	Living Waters	Telling the Stories of our Meals	Our Experiences of the Reign of God: Diversity
Session #2 Creativity in the Hebrew Scriptures	The Community Tells Its Stories of Creation: Genesis	Created for Places of Promise	Creating a People: Exodus	Created as a People Who Thirst	Created as a People Who Hunger	Co-Creating the Reign of God: Who Is In, Who Is Out?
Session #3 Love in the Christian Scriptures	Stories of Loving in John	Gathered to be a Community of Boundless Compassion	Church Built on Forgiving-Love: Matthew	Washed by Waters of Love: Mark	Love Known in Sharing a Meal: Acts	Anointed in Love: The Reign of God in Luke
Session #4 Liberty in the Saints of History	Being Set Free: Absalom Jones & Dorothy Day	Gathered to Be Free in Christ: Paul of Tarsus & Harriet Tubman	The Sacred Journey: Brigid & Brendan	Wading into the Waters: Sojourner Truth & Dag Hammarskjöld	Free to Eat, Free to Labor: Caesar Chavez & Elizabeth of Hungary	Celebrating & Serving God's Reign: Frederick Douglas & Eleanor Roosevelt
Session #5 Restorative Justice & Community	Creating Our Story of Restorative Justice	Gathered as a Sign of Justice	Sent to Heal	River of Renewal	Caring : Welcoming to the Table	Everyone Belongs: The Reign of God
Session #6	Review & Celebrate	Review & Celebrate	Review & Celebrate	Review & Celebrate	Review & Celebrate	Review & Celebrate
Spiritual Practices	Daily Devotions The Offices	Journaling Canticles	Collects	Symbolic Action	Thanksgiving & Graces	Intercessory Prayer
Tools of the Trade	Biblical Overview	Scripture Translations	J,E,D,P	Gospel Parallels	Literary Devices	Types of Literature
Leadership Skills	Inclusion	Asking questions	Setting boundaries	Giving and receiving feedback	Caring vs. therapy	Supporting diversity

The full scope & sequence, as well as free sample pages are available at www.LeaderResources.org

RULE OF LIFE

Description: A Rule of Life is a description of the direction a person or congregation feels called by God to pursue. The scope is greater than particular goals, but articulates the general bearing and areas to explore. A congregational Rule of Life may come out of the work done by a congregational formation process.

Format: The form a communal Rule of Life takes will reflect the relationship the community has with God. The 12 Steps of AA are a good model to look at when considering writing a Rule of Life. I have also reprinted below an example of a Rule of Life put together by St. Stephen's Episcopal Church in Casper, WY. St. Stephen's created this Rule after a going through the "Rooted in God" formation process. They now use it to direct their planning and their life together, projecting it on the wall every Sunday after worship.

Indications for Use: Writing a Rule of Life helps a congregation define not only who they are, but who they feel called to become. The scope of the Rule is broad, so that yearly goals can be set as needs arise and membership changes. The Rule however, keeps the community moving over many years in a particular direction.

A Rule of life will also provide a way to evaluate your congregation's progress. In evaluation, the Rule can be referred to as the members reflect on the ministries and mission they have undertaken. The word "rule" here is does not mean an iron clad order, but rather a guiding map to keep the focus of the congregation on God's call.

Cautions: For a Rule of Life to be helpful in the congregational setting, the majority of members must have their fingerprints on it in some way. Otherwise, it is not a discipline freely accepted, but an imposed order. While the involvement of members may come at different stages and in different ways, it is important not to hurry through the process of creating a Rule of Life.

If a Rule of Life is embraced by a congregation, it must also be widely publicized and often referred to so that it continues to be a relevant reference point. Continued sharing of the Rule at meetings and Sunday worship also helps newcomers understand the church and invites their buy-in as they consider joining the congregation.

St Stephen's Rule of Life

We commit ourselves to be involved in all aspects of church life:
  Liturgy
  Pastoral Care
  Evangelism/Mission
  Vision
  Administration

We commit ourselves to encourage each other to use our spiritual gifts.

We commit ourselves to create an environment where groups and individuals are invited to explore and define their spirituality by asking, listening, and learning from each other and from God.

We commit ourselves to the stability, growth and transformation of St. Stephen's by working together and by our commitment to God.

MUTUAL MINISTRY REVIEW

Description: Evaluation of the process of development is an essential element both for learning as we go and for holding ourselves accountable for the ministries to which we are committed. The Mutual Ministry Review provides a way for the whole congregation to come together for evaluation on a regular basis, usually annually.

Format: Mutual Ministry Reviews are done in one or a series of meetings. They are exercises structured to give equal voice to many viewpoints and to critique the ministries which are being done by the congregation. The goal of the review is not to cast blame for problems, but to name both areas of strength and weakness honestly and seek a way forward into greater maturity as a Christian community.

Indications: In many congregations, the review is done by the governing board with results presented to the congregation. However, in Mutual Ministry congregations it is important for everyone to learn the art of critical review and analysis, while supporting the evolving community. Consider holding a Mutual Ministry Review as part of the annual meeting of the church and invite as many people as possible to participate.

Cautions: There is always a temptation (especially when things are difficult) to scapegoat a person or group of people. The attitude which must prevail when a Mutual Ministry Review is undertaken is one of unity: "We are in this together and God has given us what we need to succeed. No one is expendable." Reminders to use techniques of conversation and dialogue (as opposed to debate) will be helpful.

Directions: Very helpful outlines and directions for Mutual Ministry Reviews can be found in the free guide "Living into Our Ministries: The Mutual Ministry Cycle" at http://www.episcopalchurch.org/documents/CDO_Living_into_our Ministries.pdf.

I have also included below a sample agenda for a brief (two hour) Mutual Ministry Review meeting.

MUTUAL MINISTRY REVIEW

SAMPLE AGENDA FOR A 2 HOUR MEETING

I)   Opening prayer and rounds:
     What I hope to get out of today's meeting is...   **15 minutes**

II) Bible Study in small groups using the Gospel Based Discipleship Bible Study
     format.   **15 minutes**

III) SWOT Exercise to analyze what's going on in the present moment.

     1 - Give each participant a stack of small sticky notes. Ask them to write (one
     to a note) their three top answers to each area of the SWOT chart:

Strength	**W**eaknesses
What is working well?	What is missing or needs improvement?
Opportunities	**T**hreats
What opportunities do you see?	What threat have you identified?)-

                                                             10-15 minutes

     2 - In plenary, put in appropriate square and group ideas that seem to go
     together.   **10-15 minutes**

     3 - Starting with Strengths:
          a - Identify common areas
          b - Analyze top three in each category on another sheet, i.e. What is
          contributing to this? What is inhibiting this? Consider Values, People,
          Structures, Pay off (benefit).

                                                             10- 15 minutes

Example: We have a great Choir

Enhancers (Blue)	Inhibitors (Red)*reverse color for W&T
Choir Director	Volunteers are not consistent
Music is important	We never pay for music
Place in worship to shine	No time on Sunday to practice
Beautiful, engaging worship	

IV)   Planning for the future.

1 - Brainstorm- Any common themes that keep cropping up in Red or Blue areas?

List on board or circle.   **10 minutes**

2 - APA analysis: What do you want to achieve, preserve, avoid? Both short term and long term?

Brainstorm with chart on board.   **20 minutes**
Produce time line of priorities: How? When? Who will lead?   **20 minutes**

V)   Closing Prayer

GIFTS DISCERNMENT WORKSHOP

Description: The goal of this workshop is to help individuals, through a group process, discover and articulate gifts they have exhibited or have the potential of developing, which could be used for ministry and mission.

Format: This 2 ½ to 3 hour workshop invites people to think about their accomplishments and then, in a small group setting, explore what gifts those actions might reveal. In the process, not only do individuals discover abilities, skills and motivations they have, but they also learn much about their fellow members… all in a supportive and encouraging atmosphere.

Indications for use: This is an exercise to be used in conjunction with the discovery of ministry roles needed in a congregation and before the calling process begins. As many people in the congregation should be included as possible, as well as any paid staff including rectors or pastors. Sharing the discovery of gifts is a step in the whole calling process.

Cautions: It may be tempting to do this step, which is so encouraging and supportive to members, early in the development process. But if it is done before a well thought out Rule of Life or other proactive plan is in place, the energy generated may be dispersed before the gifts discovered can be called upon. Discouragement, and even cynical disbelief of the intention of inviting the use of everyone's talents, can set in if the results of the workshop are set aside and forgotten.

Directions: An agenda for the Gifts Discernment Workshop is included below, along with instructions and a worksheet. I offer it with this note of attribution: I can't remember where I first experienced the core of this workshop and I have been modifying it for at least twenty years. I received the idea from some source I no longer recall, but for whom I am thankful!

GIFTS DISCERNMENT WORKSHOP EXAMPLE

SAMPLE AGENDA

Materials needed:
- Gifts/Skills/Talents Identification worksheets for all
- Poster size paper for each small group
- pens/pencils for all
- Markers for each group

I.   Bible Study   **10 minutes**

II.   Introduction to workshop   15 **minutes**

    Points to make about Gift Discernment:
- Gifts, when exercised, bring joy!
- Gifts are meant to be used for the building up of community.
- Gifts must be trained
- Discernment of gifts is an ongoing process of discovery.
- Everyone has at least one gift.
- Beware of danger of projection, i.e. thinking a gift which comes easily to you should be available to everyone else.
- Ministry descriptions are necessary to be sure that gifts are assigned to the right task and avoid burnout

III.   Instruct everyone to do Steps 1-3 by themselves (see "Instructions below)
Go over worksheet (also below).   **20 minutes**

IV.   Leader: Role play step 4 with someone else discerning the skills & talents inherent in achievements.   **5 minutes**

V.   Groups do step 4 with each person sharing achievements A, B, and C while other members help the individual think about the skills and talents he/she has to accomplish such an achievement.   **30-40 minutes**

VI.   Small groups share with whole the gifts they have discovered. Allow others in the large group to add additional gifts to any of the names.   **20 minutes**

VII   Debrief (How did this feel? What was helpful? How can we use this info?)
                                                                            10 minutes

VIII.   Closing Prayer

Instructions

1.   Range through your memory and think of several achievement experiences – those you feel were most significant in your life. Write down a few words to describe each. Do it for at least seven achievements in the boxes on the other side of this paper.

2.   Check five achievements you feel were your greatest.

3.   Prioritize those five: "A" is greatest of all, "B" is second, and so on.

4.   Start with achievement "A". Recall carefully what you did to make this happen. Let others in your group ask questions to help focus your memories. In the Gifts/Skills/Talents column, write down the skills and talents you must have applied to achievement "A". In the last column record any motivations you can remember.

5.   Do the same recalling and skills identification for the B and C achievements. See which skills/talents and motivations you have used repeatedly to make the different experiences happen. These repeated elements are your strengths or energies that can become the foundation for your ministry!

Achievements	Skills/Talents/Gifts	Motivation

MINISTRY ROLE DESCRIPTION

Description: The Ministry Role Description articulates a job or role in the church and spells out the expectations of the community, along with the commitments of support and training which will be provided.

Format: Ministry Role Descriptions are written after a Rule of Life or long-range plan have been created for the congregation. New or existing ministries which will support the church's progress in their proactive plan will then need to be articulated and leaders identified.

Areas to consider in a MRD include long range goals for the job as well as specific tasks, the type of leadership style needed, gifts and talents, and the people this person will interact with for support and evaluation. It also is important to spell out how much time will be required and the length of commitment. Training and other resources should also be noted.

While the creation of the MRDs belong to the whole congregation, it is best to give the initial drafting to several small teams, who can then bring their proposed drafts back for editing and approval by the whole.

Indications for use: The creation of MRDs gives structure and focus to the calling process that will help even the smallest congregation be more successful in recognizing who is best for what role. It also is invaluable for delineating responsibilities and time required, which in turn makes it possible for harried and over-burdened member to know exactly what they are committing to. If burn-out has been a problem, MRDs can remind members of the parameters of their responsibilities.

Cautions: The writing of MRDs is time consuming. Distribute the responsibility so no one has to do too many. And remind people that this is not a job description. It can be more of an outline, with details to be filled in by the people actually doing the work.

Description: Below is a sample of a Ministry Role Description for a Ministry Support Team Member. Notice how brief and general it is, while clearly spelling out time commitments and training support.

MINISTRY ROLE DESCRIPTION SAMPLE

Ministry Description: Ministry Support Team (MST)

Goals:
- growth of church/individuals;
- coordinate – coagulate – gel –
- involve more individuals
- accountability/communication among teams

Tasks:
- communicate with other team leaders
- hold each other accountable
- recognize growth and celebrate
- set goals
- review changes to ministry descriptions
- imagine/dream out life together
- plan for ongoing discernment

Leadership Type: big picture and bridge builder

Contact People: whole church, vestry, ministry developer

Spiritual Gifts: creativity, patience, organization, enthusiasm, listening/communicating, prayerful, optimism, supportive, open

Abilities: collaboration, seeing big picture, organized, see outside the box, open minded, flexibility, perseverance

Time: 4-6 hours per month

Length: 1 year

Training: diocese, Lifecycles, OJT ("on-the-job training")

CONGREGATIONAL CALLING WORKSHOP

Definition: The congregational calling workshop is an exercise in discernment for the whole congregation. It seeks to structure calling for ministry roles in an interaction between what is known about the gifts of members and what is known about the needs of the church, with a room for inspiration and freedom of choice. It opens up the process of discernment to everyone involved.

This workshop was designed for (and perhaps works best with) small congregations, where the whole membership can be gathered into one room. Its principles, however, will be sound for larger churches as well. The workshop could be broken down into two parts: The first act would be the gathering of names under the various headings of gifts for ministry, which could be done in a parish hall over a number of weeks. The second act could be the division of areas of call corresponding to the subjects on the Rule of Life or long-range plan, which might then be addressed at different times and places with leaders already responsible for those areas.

Format: The workshop as presented below will take about three hours for a small congregation to complete. It is dependent on having both individual members' gifts identified already and ministry role descriptions written. No specialized leadership is required. However, good conversational skills and a time keeper will help move the workshop along.

Indications for use: In striving towards Mutual Ministry, it is important to involve as many people as possible in the calling process and still have carefully considered discernment. This workshop seeks to find that balance. Congregations may want to consider using it on a regular basis, to keep discernment and calling fresh and available to all members.

Cautions: The success of this workshop is dependent on 1) having members aware of their gifts and talents and 2) having the congregation clear on the ministry roles to which they will be calling people. It should not be attempted without these two things already in place.

Encourage members to only accept two or three calls. To commit to more not only puts stress on the member accepting these calls, it takes away another's chance to play a significant role.

CONGREGATIONAL CALLING WORKSHOP EXAMPLE

SAMPLE AGENDA

Goal: To create the environment and structure in which members of the congregation can call and be called to ministry roles in the church.

Materials Needed:
- Already filled-in Ministry Role Descriptions
- Poster sized paper with the headings of gift "categories" on the wall.
- Members' lists of gifts discovered at the Gifts Discernment Workshop
- Rule of Life flow chart
- Pencils and paper
- Tripod, pad and markers
- Directories

Preparation: Before the workshop, put up poster sized paper around the room with headings of various categories of spiritual gifts. Members will put their names below these headings if they have a discovered that they either have or have the potential for developing a similar gift. Keep in mind that the naming of gifts is an inexact science. What one person has called "hospitality" another may call "making people comfortable" or "entertaining". Try to be clear about the parameters of the gift you have listed on the headings, so people will know where their name belongs.

Remind people to bring their results from the Gifts Discernment Workshop with them. If you have some participants today who were not present at the discernment workshop, let them make the best guess they can for where their names should go.

Remind people that this is not an exact science. All we do here today is to help us focus on the task of calling and to be open to the Holy Spirit among us.

I.   An Opening prayer:

"O God, by whom the meek are guided in judgment, and light rises up in
darkness for the godly: Grant us, in all our doubts and uncertainties, the grace
to ask what you would have us to do the Spirit of wisdom may save us from all
false choices, and that in your light we may see light, and in your straight path
may not stumble; through Jesus Christ our Lord. Amen"[70] (BCP 832)

II.   Individuals' Exercise:

On the sheets of paper on the wall: List yourself (and anyone who has not
been a part of the previous workshop but you identified as having a particular
gift) below the headings which describe your gifts.. Include both gifts you
already use and those for which you have great potential.   **15 minutes**

III.   In plenary:

Go over the areas of the Rule of Life (or other long-range proactive plan)
which were created. Describe the roles which have been identified as
necessary to grow in those areas.   **15 minutes**

IV.   Divide into self-selected small groups around Rule of Life areas. Give each
group the Ministry Descriptions that fit their subject.   **40-60 minutes**

Small group Exercise:

Taking one Ministry Role Description at a time, review the Abilities/Spiritual
Gifts listed for that role.

Review the list of names appearing under the Spiritual Gifts (specified for that
particular Role) on the sheets around the room and discuss the possibility of
those people who have one or two matches being called to that ministry.
(If there is not an exact match use the ones that match most closely. Pay
attention to heart and gut feelings here, as well as your heads!)

Decide who you would like to ask to take on the ministry roles being
considered by your group. Consider both actual and potential gifts and
interests etc. You may suggest more than one name for each role, as those
people discerned will also have the opportunity to accept or decline. In many

roles, it would not be bad to have more than one person committed to the ministry.

V.   **In Plenary:** Share results of the small groups' deliberation, one small group report at a time.   **50 minutes**

Ask for feedback from those individuals called. There are three appropriate responses: 1) Yes, this is something I will do. 2) Maybe. I need to think and pray about it, 3) No, this is not at all what I feel called to at this time.

Assign a small group of people to follow through with members who answered "maybe", with prayer and dialogue. Another group may be assigned to visit and offer calls to people not in attendance. (This period of extended discernment should be no more than two weeks.)

Set date when this round of discernment will end and the ministry leadership roles will be assigned and announced.

VII   Debrief: How did this feel? What was helpful?   **10 minutes**

VIII   Closing Prayer

ENDNOTES

CHAPTER 1

[1] *The Book of Common Prayer*, (New York, NY: The Church Pension Fund, 1986). Pp. 304-305.
[2] David Paton and Chares H. Long ed.s, *The Compulsion of the Spirit: A Roland Allen Reader* (Grand Rapids: William B. Eerdmans Publ. Co. and Cincinnati, Ohio: Forward Movement Publications, 1983) See especially Chapter 2.
[3] Robin Greenwood and Caroline Pascoe, ed.s, *Local Ministry: Story, Process and Meaning* (London, England: Society for Promoting Christian Knowledge, 2006) p.84. While I'm not sure where this pithy motto comes from, a longer version is quoted in Rob Daborn's chapter as originating from Tim Dearborn.
[4] Christopher Duraisingh, "From Church-Shaped Mission to Mission-Shaped Church," *Anglican Theological Review*, Winter, 2010, p. 9.
[5] Sheryl Kujawa-Holbrook and Fredrica Harris Thompsett, *Born of Water, Born of Spirit: Supporting the Ministry of the Baptized in Small Congregations* (Herndon, VA: The Alban Institute, 2010).

CHAPTER 2

[6] Peter Senge, The Fifth Discipline: The Art and Practice of The Learning Organization (New York, New York: Currency Doubleday, 1990) p. 240.
[7] *Ibid.* p. 10.
[8] Margaret Wheatley, *Turning to One Another: Simple Conversations to Restore Hope to the Future* (San Francisco: Berrett-Koehler, Publishers, Inc., 2002) p.29.
[9] Mike Mather, Vital Ministry in the Small-Membership Church: Sharing Stories, Shaping Community (Nashville, TN: Discipleship Resources, 2002) pp.29-30.
[10] From conversations with The Rev. Kathy Robinson, Episcopal Diocese of Wyoming
[11] Peter Senge, The Fifth Discipline: The Art and Practice of The Learning Organization (New York, New York: Currency Doubleday, 1990) p. 64.
[12] Peter Schwartz, *The Art of the Long View: Planning for the Future in an Uncertain World* (New York, New York: Currency Doubleday Publishers, 1991) p. 3.

CHAPTER 3

[13] Margaret Wheatley, *Finding Our Way: Leadership for an Uncertain Time* (San Francisco: Berrett-Koehler Publishers, Inc., 2005) p. 86.
[14] Ibid., p. 28.
[15] Peter Senge, Bryn Smith, Nina Kruschwitz, Joe Laur, Sara Schley, *The Necessary Revolution: How Individuals and Organizations are Working together to Create a Sustainable World* (New York: Doubleday, 2008) Kindle Location 3794-99.
[16] Peter Senge, Art Kleiner, Charlotte Roberts, Richard B. Ross, and Bryn J. Smith, *The Fifth Discipline Fieldbook: Strategies and Tools for Building a Learning Organization* (New York: Doubleday, 1994) pp. 256-259.

[17] Margaret Wheatley, *Finding Our Way: Leadership for an Uncertain* Time (San Francisco: Berrett-Koehler Publishers, Inc., 2005) p. 28.

CHAPTER 4

[18] Eugene H. Peterson, *The Message: The Bible in Contemporary Language* (Colorado Springs, Colorado: NavPress, 2002), p. 2084.

[19] Stuart Kaufman, *At Home in the Universe* (New York, NY: Oxford University Press, 1995), p. 274.

[20] Margaret Wheatley, *Leadership and the New Science* (San Francisco, CA: Berrett-Koehler Publishers, Inc., 1992), p. 94.

[21] Wheatley, Leadership and the New Science, p. 135.

[22] Roy M. Oswald and Robert E Friedrich, Jr., *Discerning Your Congregation's Future: A Strategic and Spiritual Approach* (New York, NY: Alban Institute, 1989), pp.79-80.

[23] Passport to the Future: How the Local Parish Can Discover its Unique Personality, 1998,Doctoral Thesis

[24] Carl Dudley and Sally A. Johnson, "Energizing the Congregation: Images that Shape Your Church's Ministry,"(Louisville, Kentucky: Westminster/John Knox Press, 1993)

CHAPTER 5

[25] Donella H. Meadows, *Thinking in Systems: A Primer* (White River Junction, Vermont: Chelsea Green Publishing, 2008), Kindle location 162.

[26] Margaret A. Babcock, *Rooted in God: Moving from Maintenance to Mission* (Leeds, MA: LeaderResources, 2005)

[27] Fredrica Harris Thompsett, *Wade in the Water (a video)* (Cambridge, MA: Episcopal Divinity School, 2007).

[28] Babcock, Rooted in God: Moving from Maintenance to Mission

[29] ibid

[30] *LifeCycles* (Leeds, MA: LeaderResources, 2002-2011)

[31] Kevin Thew Forrester, *I Have Called You Friends: An Invitation to Ministry* (New York, NY: Church Publishing Inc., 2003)

[32] Robert Linthicum, *Transforming Power: Biblical Strategies for Making a Difference in Your Community* (Downers Grove, IL: InterVarsity Press, 2003)

CHAPTER 6

[33] Gerald Harris, *The Art of Quantum Planning: Lessons from Quantum Physics for Breakthrough Strategy, Innovation, and Leadership,* (San Francisco, CA: Berrett-Koehler Publishers, Inc., 2009) Kindle location #805.

[34] Samuel P. Magill, *Living into Our Ministries: The Mutual Ministry Cycle, A Resource Guide* (New York, New York: The Episcopal Church Foundation, 2003) http://www.episcopalchurch.org/documents/CDO_Living_Into_Our_Ministries.pdf

[35] Sue Annis Hammond, *The Thin Book of Appreciative Inquiry* (Bend, OR: Thin Book Publishing Co.,1996) Kindle location #270.

[36] Ibid. Kindle location #287.

[37] Peter Schwartz, *The Art of the Long View: Paths to Strategic Insight for Yourself and Your Company* (New York, NY: Bantam Doubleday Bell Publishing Group, Inc., 1991).

[38] Ibid. *The Art of Quantum Planning* (quoted from Arie P. de Geus, "Planning as Learning" Harvard Business Review, March and April 1988), Kindle location # 123.

CHAPTER 7

[39] Peter M. Senge, *The Fifth Discipline: The Art and Practice of the Learning Organization,* (New York, New York: Bantam Doubleday Dell Publ., 1990) p. 8.

[40] Sue Annis Hammond and Andrea B. Mayfield, *The Thin Book of Naming Elephants: How to Surface Undiscussables for Greater Organizational Success,* Kindle Edition (Bend, OR: Thin Book Publishing, 2004) Chapter 2, Section on "Constructive Dialogue" locations 279-88.

[41] Christian A. Schwartz, *The Three Colors of Ministry,* pp. 64-85 (St. Charles, IL: Church Smart Resources, 2001)

[42] Br. Lawrence was a Carmelite lay brother in the 17th century who became a great spiritual director out of his simple and insightful sharing of his relationship with God. His letters are recorded in *The Practice of the Presence of God,* now in the public domain and available through the Gutenberg Press project.

[43] Schwartz, *The Three Colors of Ministry,* p. 155.

[44] *Education For Ministry,* (Sewanee, TN: The University of the South, 1984)

[45] *LifeCycles,* (Leeds, MA: LeaderResources, 2002-2011)

CHAPTER 8

[46] Fredrick Buechner, *Wishful Thinking: A Seeker's ABC,* (by San Francisco, CA: Harper, 1973)

[47] Eugene H. Peterson, *The Message: The New Testament in Contemporary Language* (Colorado Springs, CO: NavPress Publishing Group, 1993) pp.62-63.

[48] Joseph Meyers, Organic Community: Creating a Place Where People Naturally Connect (Grand Rapids, MI: Baker Publishing Group, 2007).

[49] Ibid., p. 140.

[50] David L. Cooperrider and Dianna Whitney, *Appreciative Inquiry: A Positive Revolution in Change* (San Francisco, CA: Berrett Koehler Publishers, Inc., 2005) Kindle location 535.

[51] See the exercise on teaching Relational Meetings in *Rooted in God,* pp.

[52] *LifeCycles* (Leeds, MA: LeaderResources, 2002-2007)

[53] *Education for Ministry* (EFM), (Sewanee, TN: The University of the South, 1984).

[54] Donella Meadows, *Thinking in Systems* (Kindle location 787 and forward)

THE TOOL SHED

[55] By Juanita Brown and the World Café Community ©2002 *Whole Systems Associates. Please feel free to reproduce with acknowledgement of* source. http://www.theworldcafe.com

[56] *Rooted in God* p.16

[57] *Rooted in God* pp.20-22

[58] *Rooted in God* p.23

[59] *Rooted in God* p.24

[60] Margaret Wheatley, *Turning to One Another: Simple Conversations to Restore Hope to the Future* (San Francisco, CA: Berrett-Koehler, Inc., 2002), p. 29.

[61] *Discerning your Congregation's Future*, Alban Institute

[62] Carl S. Dudley and Sally A. Johnson, *Energizing the Congregation: Images That Shape Your Church's Ministry* (Louisville, Kentucky: Westminster/John Knox Press, 1993).

[63] Margaret A. Babcock, *Passport to the Future: How the Local Parish Can Discover Its Unique Personality* (Evanston IL: Seabury-Western Theological Seminary, 1998).

[64] Dudley and Johnson, *Energizing the Congregation*, passim. The way these five types of churches would answer is gleaned directly from Dudley and Johnson's discussion of each type. These discussions range throughout the book.

[65] Ibid., p.6.

[66] Ibid.

[67] Sue Annis Hammond, *The Thin Book of Appreciative Inquiry* (Bend, OR: Thin Book Publishing, 1996)

[68] David L. Cooperrider and Diana Whitney, *Appreciative Inquiry: A Positive Revolution in Change* (San Francisco, CA: Berrett Koehler Publishers, Inc., 2005)

[69] James D. Ludema, Diana Whitney, Bernard J. Mohr and Thomas J. Griffin, *The Appreciative Inquiry Summit: A Practitioner's Guide for Leading Large-Group Change* (San Francisco, CA: Berrett Koehler Publishers, Inc., 2003)

[70] *The Book of Common Prayer*, (New York, NY: The Church Pension Fund, 1986) p.832.

ABOUT THE AUTHOR

The Rev. Margaret Babcock is an ordained Episcopal priest with 20 years of congregational ministry and 10 years of experience at the judicatory level as Canon for Ministry and Congregational Development in the dioceses of Idaho and Wyoming. She is author of the program "Rooted in God: Moving from Maintenance to Mission" published by LeaderResources.

Margaret holds an MDiv from Seabury-Western Theological Seminary, as well as a DMin in Congregational Development. She also has a community counseling MS degree from Mankato State University. Margaret currently resides in Casper, WY and is the director of Companion Way Consulting Services which seeks to support both congregational and judicatory development in a Mutual Ministry style.

Made in the USA
Lexington, KY
09 May 2014